S0-AXK-898

BORN TO PUN

BORN TO PUN

1,400 BOSS JOKES, FUNNY QUIPS AND **GROAN-WORTHY** PUNCHLINES!

Gordon Hideaki Nagai

Ulysses Press

Text copyright © 2018 Gordon Hideaki Nagai. Design and concept
copyright © 2018 Ulysses Press and its licensors. All rights reserved.
Any unauthorized duplication in whole or in part or dissemination of
this edition by any means (including but not limited to photocopying,
electronic devices, digital versions, and the internet) will be prosecuted to
the fullest extent of the law.

Published in the U.S. by
ULYSSES PRESS
P.O. Box 3440
Berkeley, CA 94703
www.ulyssespress.com

ISBN: 978-1-61243-788-0
Library of Congress Control Number 2018930757

10 9 8 7 6 5 4 3 2 1

Printed in the U.S. by Kingery Printing Company, United Graphics Division

Acquisitions editor: Casie Vogel
Managing editor: Claire Chun
Editor: Shayna Keyles
Proofreader: Darcy Reed
Front cover design: Justin Shirley
Cover artwork: © gulserinak1955/shutterstock.com

Distributed by Publishers Group West

IMPORTANT NOTE TO READERS: This book is independently authored and
published. No endorsement or sponsorship by or affiliation with movies,
celebrities, products, or other copyright and trademark holders is claimed
or suggested. All references in this book to copyrighted or trademarked
characters and other elements of movies and products are for the purpose of
commentary, criticism, analysis, and literary discussion only.

To all the dads who over the years have
fractured French, thrashed Thai, garbled German, and
murdered the English language in order to serve up those
maddening plays on words that have generally entertained
and ravaged our lives—We can't tank you enough!

CONTENTS

INTRODUCTION

Words, words, words!

Is a picture, as the Chinese saying goes, worth a thousand words? And is the reverse also true, that one word is worth a thousand pictures? What is one word worth? Would William Wordsworth have wondered the same?

Words are portals to a realm within each of us where dwell creatures monstrous and terrifying, and others delicate and wondrous and universally healing. It is a world to which, as children, we had ready access to, and where we spent lengthy periods in active make believe. It is the cauldron where dreams and spirit and all creativity are born. It is where the fires of valor are stoked that enable us to rise up and, when need be, reach beyond our limits. And it is because of the nature of words that this world is opened.

Enter the artist as dream weaver: From that first creative soul who daubed pigments and charcoal images on the walls of caves to those who beat out the tempo to which they alone march, artists are the bellwether of the human race. They give us a window onto our past and intimations of our future. Is it any wonder then that they have strummed the rhythmic chords within us that cause us to dance?

It is said that puns are an art form, though they are, in our cultural parlance, generally considered the stepchild of real art. However, they are considered by others to be the most sophisticated of the arts, and they are available to and accessible by anyone with a fair degree of mastery over language. That an immigrant with only rudimentary skills with English can enjoy puns speaks to their powers to excite.

And it doesn't require genius to generate puns, only a grasp of language and a willingness to suspend the lockstep rules of language and meaning and to risk wonder and the unexpected.

There is a fascinating word for all this: *paronomasia*, the use of words to make puns. Thus, a *paronomasiac* is one who loves and conjures puns. In our more free moments, we recognize that puns are an acquired taste that has to have groan on you over the years. (Sorry! I couldn't help myself!)

The jokes, puns, and "dad jokes" in this volume are the fruits of a bent mind, one with its roots in that early childhood realm of make-believe. It was sheltered as I grew through my teen years into adulthood. While others left this world behind as they grew up, I clandestinely kept contact with and nurtured it, spending time in reverie, as most introverts do.

It is with pleasure that I present these groan-worthy tidbits for your consumption. If I am able to elicit a roll of the eyes or a slap of the forehead with a stifled smirk, I have accomplished my mission here.

Whatever your idea of how the world works, or should, enjoy your stint through this mind field of Cracker Jacks prizes.

CHAPTER ONE
SCHOOL

The fraternity student ended up in the university's hospital when he was injured trying to surf "the wave" at the football game.

When the English teacher vacationed at a state park, he drove past tents before finding his campsite.

The cheerleading squad came under criticism for having uniforms considered too revealing, but with a few modifications, they skirted further difficulties.

When the marionette earned a degree in theoretical physics, he decided to specialize in the study of string theory.

The son of the translator for the deaf came home from school all excited because he learned how to sign the "F" word.

When the young man graduated from Shepherd School, he looked for a staff position on a farm.

The young man's parents were so proud when he graduated from Shepherd School, they framed his sheepskin.

The entrepreneurial graduate from the Shepherd School started a business of crooks.

The university's track coach is renowned for "running" a high-powered athletic program.

The graduate of the prestigious Shepherd School ran into trouble keeping track of his flock. Every time he took to counting his sheep, he dropped off to sleep.

The president of the Shepherd Academy decided he would flock all the Christmas trees for the holidays.

Improper use of punctuation can lead to a comma-tose state for some English teachers.

Are alumni who give large sums of money to a university's football program thought of as athletic supporters?

To join the fraternity of vampire brothers, one has to swear a blood oath.

There is an entrance exam for barber college designed to see if you can cut it.

The curriculum at the barber college doesn't just include professional techniques, but also a study of the history and hairitage of the profession.

It got the attention of all the fathers in the class when the professor announced a pop quiz for Friday.

A significant portion of a civil engineer's education and training centers around concrete principles of design.

Many civil engineers become Roads Scholars.

When the young man graduated from Shepherd School, he was just glad to get the flock out.

The Shepherd School was so famous that students flocked to get in.

The Shepherd School closed down temporarily because some crooks were involved in a scandal.

Shepherd School graduates do well in life because they learn how to take good care of ewe.

Shepherd School students love wool gathering because of the shear joy of the work.

The young and naïve Shepherd School student learned a valuable lesson when an unscrupulous card player fleeced him.

The orthopedic medical student thought his finals would be a snap as long as he did a little boning-up.

Upon graduation all Shepherd School students receive the sheepskin documenting their achievement.

The pretty, young history teacher asked her student about a historic date, and he got the wrong idea.

When chickens become educators, they rarely have trouble with teaching eggsamples.

The chicken dean of students was harsh when eggscoriating pranksters who'd cracked a few too many yolks.

Medical schools seek to discourage orthopedic surgeons from having knee-jerk reactions to obvious health conditions.

The medical student knew he wanted to be an orthopedic surgeon from when he was in knee pants.

The class of orthopedic surgeons will have a class clown known for his penchant for ribbing everyone.

When marionettes take drama in school, the key is learning how to relax and hang loose.

First year orthopedic medical students maintain a skeletal class schedule because of their arduous studies.

The med student, in preparing for her exam to become a licensed orthopedic surgeon, reviewed that the leg bone is connected to the anklebone...

When the alarm sounded, the chicken student body quickly eggsited the building.

When the geometry teacher found herself involved in a love triangle, she was upset and wanted to square things with both men.

The geometry teacher started a new pizza business trying something innovative: each pi had four sides so customers could get a square meal.

Immediately upon graduating, cartographers begin mapping out their futures.

It's a rare cartographer who, upon graduating, doesn't have a direction in their life.

The impostor orthopedic surgeon had multiple degrees attesting to his status as a boneified medical professional, but they were all fakes.

Ms. Smith, 4th period English, gave me my gold shield as a Grammar Detective. My charge: Go after all bad punktuation.

The English teacher got a call from the Grammar Police when she used an incorrect word. She should have noun better.

The young barber college student didn't graduate with his class because he cut too many of his classes.

Some parents were concerned the cheerleader's outfits were too form-fitting and suggestive, but the girls felt they should just loosen up a little.

The cheerleaders' uniforms were tight with a bare midriff because they felt it would be a waist of effort otherwise in their routines.

When parents are so concerned about the tight-fitting outfits worn by today's cheerleaders they forget the brief history of their own indiscretions.

All this discussion and controversy over the skimpiness of outfits worn by cheerleaders is overblown and that's the long and short of it.

The parents of the graduate of the Shepherd Academy were so proud of their son, for a graduation present they gave him a Dodge Ram pickup.

For his doctoral thesis in the graduate school of the Shepherd Academy the student wrote on the topic, "The Shear Pleasures of Raising Sheep."

The recent graduate of the Shepherd Academy had a tough time getting employment and took a temporary job herding a flock of pigeons. Having no useful knowledge of birds, he had to wing it.

When the student of Shepherd Academy graduated school, he earned pocket money fleecing other students.

You wouldn't know it by just looking, but marionettes are highly educated experts in the science of string theory.

The eccentric instructor was let go by the Shepherd Academy because he acknowledged he liked to have his students follow him around like sheep.

When the triplets, Two, To, and Too, took tests in school, teachers often thought they were copying off each other.

No graduate of the Shepherd Academy is ever troubled with insomnia. You can count on it.

Cheerleading at sporting events has its roots in ancient times when young maidens danced naked to incite young lads to properly send them off to fight the tribe's wars. That's a brief history of it.

When the English teacher's husband forgot their anniversary, he suffered the shock of present tense.

When the head cheerleader was asked why the girls wear such revealing outfits she said, "It's really not very complicated, so let me be brief."

Shakespeare's teachers were not a generous bunch. When he decided he wanted to be a playwright, they thought it was a bard idea.

The controversy of the scanty outfits cheerleaders wear is because parents are concerned their daughters want to make a good showing.

The boys fully support the girl cheerleaders wearing brief revealing outfits, but the concerned parents want to get to the bottom of it all.

The ancient Babylonians, Mayans, and Indians are attributed as creators of the mathematical concept of "zero." The world still applauds them for making such a fuss about nothing.

English teachers would like to impose a sintax for poor grammar.

The surgeon was a former student of the English teacher, who elected to be put into an induced comma during the operation.

The young, virtuous student was reluctant to learn how to write in cursive because he thought it had to do with profanity and swearing.

In grade school I learned that the zero was considered a placeholder, but it didn't count for anything.

The three brothers, See, Sea, and Si, had very different life stories: One studied and became an ophthalmologist, one joined the navy, and the youngest moved to Spain.

The doctoral student's math thesis was on an aspect of the binary number system but she found that half of her work added up to nothing.

When I was a teenager, I thought my math teacher had a great figure.

Are math teachers in Italy called Pi-sans?

Are math teachers who take up flying called pi-lots?

The geometry teacher wanted to take a break in her relationship because she wanted to have her own space.

Geometry teachers try to go around in the best of circles.

When her friends broke up, the geometry teacher tried not to take sides.

The geometry teacher loved to sun bathe at the beach and watch all the tan gents walk by.

The calculus teacher secured a bank loan to buy her first home but had to have someone cosine the contract with her.

When the geometry teacher got married, the ceremony was with just a close circle of friends.

The meteorologist graduated Magna Cum Laude with a Fahrenheit degree.

The English professor had a novel idea for a story made up of short, choppy sentences. It turned out to be a period piece.

When chickens take a typing class, they rarely get beyond the hunt-and-peck method.

In the beginning, the hunt-and-peck system of typing had been perfected by chicken secretarial schools, but it is now generally considered a fowl system.

When the woodpecker attended the Hunt-and-Peck Secretarial Academy she excelled and could peck a record-high 150 words per minute.

The graduate student's doctoral dissertation at the Shepherd Academy was titled "Sleep Inducing Techniques: A Program You Can Count on."

Students in advanced orthopedic surgery programs are generally poor and have personal budgets pared down to the bone.

The chicken bully got a taste of her own medicine when her classmates started calling her a dumb cluck.

When Jack Rabbit graduated from medical school, his chosen specialty was anesthesiology because he wanted to be an Ether Bunny.

The teacher sent the obnoxious parrot to the principal's office for mocking her.

It is my understanding that chicken secretarial schools teach a strict hunt-and-peck system.

CHAPTER TWO

WORK

The professional football player-turned-ventriloquist had a short learning curve when it came to throwing his voice.

Standup comedians understand that puns are an acquired taste. They'll use them sparingly and sandwich them between longer jokes.

In order to succeed as a performer, a striptease artist has to ensure her audience is pleased with her body of work.

With his knee bones so shattered, the orthopedic surgeon didn't have a leg to stand on.

The orthopedic surgeon went on a massive weight-loss regimen and lost so much weight, he ended up a mere skeleton of his former self.

An orthopedic surgeon's resumé is her bone-fides.

A knife sharpener's work can be a real grind.

You think you have it rough? Working in the sandpaper business can really wear on you.

Working in the sandpaper manufacturing business has a way of grinding you down.

The union negotiator for the sandpaper company approached contract discussions with an eye toward smoothing things over.

Working in the sandpaper manufacturing business takes true grit.

Because of his excellent reputation, the podiatrist was considered a shoe-in for the contract with the new health center.

When the dermatologist's business started to fail, he had only pore excuses to offer.

When the striptease artist added a standup comedy routine to her show, it elicited peels of laughter.

As the striptease artist approached retirement, she thought a career in politics might just suit her because she's always been in favor of transparency.

What about telemarketers, do they use sell phones to make their calls?

The EMT workers revived the heart attack victim after he'd suffered a stroke of bad luck.

When the worker's union voted to strike at the Caterpillar plant, management accused them of being distractors.

After six months on the picket lines, the union workers at the Caterpillar plant felt there was little traction in the negotiations.

Things got a little tense at the station after the meteorologist misread information about the hurricane. "I blew it!" he explained.

Grammar Police take their jobs seriously, a trait that most often spells success.

When dealing with pronouns, Grammar Police often find that it's just a matter of mistaken identity.

The sales representative for the smart phone company was arrested for possessing large amounts of company merchandise with the intent to cell.

Window cleaners on tall high-rise buildings often encounter problems; they're considered to be a pain in the glass.

The new young hire was clueless and thoroughly embarrassed when she showed up wearing a bikini on her first day in the secretarial pool.

In the lingerie business, designers of brassieres think of themselves as the industry's support group.

The operators of the concession stands in the old time drive-ins readily knew which drink was the favorite by taking a straw poll.

You don't have to have backbone to be a chiropractor, but it helps to hold the business up.

Give a sailor a length of rope and he'll be tied up in knots for hours.

Drivers of big rig 18-wheelers are very popular. You can tell by their big following.

The writer decided he wanted to write a fantasy story about a young girl and a unicorn, but knowing little about either, it turned out to be a mythtake.

The young entrepreneur was convinced it was a good idea to start a perfume business because it made scents.

When your old car has put in many good years of service and your tires show it, it's time to put it aside and retire.

Retirement allows you to couch your days in any way you want, so relax into it.

When the young couple was told starting a nursery was a daunting business venture, they ignored the advice and rose to the occasion.

When the egocentric doctor went into private practice, it was no surprise when his business failed—he didn't have the patients.

Any time a surveyor starts a new job, they strive to do their level best.

A locksmith's job is the key to everything.

In terms of providing a sense of security, a locksmith has a lock on the business.

The locksmith's business had been in the family going on several generations. The grandfather passed on a lock of his heir.

The egocentric ophthalmologist's business wasn't doing well because he had an "I" problem.

Attorneys are at higher risk of becoming alcoholics because they take their licensing exam at a bar.

Plumbers are truly fortunate: Every job is a plumb assignment.

When the plumber stopped taking his medications, he went plumb crazy.

Carpenters are truly amazing: What other job could you have where you can nail it while being hammered?

Meteorologists don't work when they're under the weather because they're not on top of it.

When the factory closed down, a lot of workers became shiftless.

If the boss calls a brief meeting, is everyone supposed to show up wearing nothing but their underwear?

Is a boss who calls brief meetings guilty of sexual harassment?

Checkmate: A pre-digital era method of paying for things.

Second Opinion: The bad choice of checking out your symptoms on the internet.

In describing their profession, do pilots use plane language?

Do locomotive engineers ever lose their train of thought?

If train engineers get drunk on the job, are they easily distrackted?

In the construction of high rises, window glass is usually the most paneful part of the budget.

The immigrant shoemaker opened a shop in the village and was the sole support for his family.

The news anchor on the network's prime time program was doing well enough that his career wasn't in danger of sinking.

Botanists love the spring. It's a time they can let their hair down and become blooming idiots.

Orthopedic surgeons preparing for any operation for injuries to the head will call together specialists for a skull session.

Orthopedic surgeons called to give expert testimony in court cases are sworn to give the bone fide truth.

Over the span of the civil engineer's career, he worked on a great many bridge projects.

Dentists and civil engineers share one thing in common: They both do bridge work.

The construction supervisor was mortarfied when the brick building collapsed because of shoddy workmanship.

The unstable meteorologist became so unprofessional, his boss had to "rain" him in.

I believe all archaeologists dig their profession.

When the company failed so spectacularly, the CEO was resigned to his fate.

The firefighter had a burning desire to do well.

An eggsterminator chicken's business is to eggstirpate a termite problem before it hatches.

A chicken sexer needs to be a skilled seggspert in order to succeed in his business.

Orthopedic surgeons are rigorous in their planning for a delicate operation and give thought to more than a skeletal plan.

In the operating room, you can easily distinguish the orthopedic surgeon by the distinctive skullcap he wears.

In their efforts to get ahead, some orthopedic surgeons have no qualms with elbowing someone aside.

Although he was the new young guy on the block, the new orthopedic surgeon was willing to shoulder the menial work assignments.

She explained to her new boyfriend that she was a radiologist at the community hospital, so when he started taking her for granted, she could see right through him.

Q: What is the all-time favorite movie of orthopedic surgeons?

A: Spinal Tap.

Orthopedic surgeons get a rush out of any spine-tingling experience.

In a misguided effort to build his practice, the orthopedic surgeon cut his service prices to the bone.

Even male cartographers won't ask directions if they get lost. It's a matter of professional pride.

Male cartographers never get lost. They may arrive late because they took the scenic route, but they never get lost.

The cartographer's mapmaking business began well, but in time, the business went south on him.

When the chicken farmer achieved a level of success, he decided to eggspand the business.

The chicken student from Italy came under an eggschange program.

When cartographers visit a place new to them, they first get the lay of the land.

A cartographer needs only two bits of information to never get lost: their phone password and the button accessing Siri.

A cartographer always knows which direction north is: it's at the top of the map.

Cartographers like to think if they refer to a topographic map, they can tell if their life is going up or down.

Cartographers like maps because they help to orient their lives.

The Red Cross chicken warden decided the eggsigent circumstances required immediate action.

After a windfall success in the stock market, the chicken farmer started to live a life of eggscess.

The chicken doctor always completed a thorough eggasamination before making her dieggnosis.

After passing his CPA exam, the man went to work for a major coffee roasting company as the head bean counter.

Being 7'10", he was well qualified to be the overseer.

To do well in his business, the introvert plumber has to pipe up when dealing with customers.

A plumber's job is often solitary, and for an introvert, that's fitting.

The arborist's business was doing so well, he decided to open a branch office.

When a plumber works under a sink, he unintentionally exposes his background.

When remodeling an older house, plumbers are often told to get the lead out.

When asked how he liked his job, Mario piped up and said that being a plumber is particularly fitting.

Considering the tools plumbers use and the contortions they sometimes have to assume, it's easy to see how they could wrench their backs.

The mattress company hired non-professionals to test their products because they wanted workers from the lay public.

The Northern Pacific Railroad hired part-time personnel to serve as semi-conductors.

The refrigerator salesman did exceedingly well because of his skills in making cold calls.

Drivers of big rig 18-wheelers are in it for the long haul.

To an obstetrician, delivering a baby is mere child's play.

The orthopedic surgeon's reason for frequenting his favorite bar is because he's all too often bone dry.

When the American Association of Orthopedic Surgeons held its annual convention on a cruise ship, everyone was bid a bone voyage.

The senior orthopedic surgeon decided it was time to retire because each day he felt weary to the bone.

In all matters of ethical concerns, the orthopedic surgeon was clearest when he felt it in his bones.

As a change of pace, the orthopedic surgeon took to writing bone-chilling crime novels.

To say the orthopedic surgeon was stubborn was to put it mildly. His colleagues felt he was just boneheaded.

Psychiatrists often delve into sailing, preferring the boat called a Freudian Sloop.

When psychiatrists venture into sailing, Jungians reject the popular Freudian Sloops in favor of shadow vessels that defy detection.

The airline pilot was a stern disciplinarian who had his whole flight team under crews control.

The landscape architect was a student of yoga. He said it grounded him.

Cardiologists are known for their excellent bedside manner. They're especially good at having heart-to-heart talks with their patients.

The barber was in a car accident and no one was hurt. He describes it as a close shave.

The butcher played a prominent role in the town because he gave everyone a nice slice of life.

The arborist's wife encouraged him to retire after a long successful career. He decided to retire and leaf the business to his son.

The pay and benefits for trash collectors can be competitive with other jobs, but the working conditions can leave some down in the dumps.

The old shipwright took on an apprentice in ship repairs and urged him to pitch right in.

The construction of the transcontinental railroad was successful because the men behind it remained focused and weren't sidetracked.

When the International Association of Orthopedic Surgeons held its annual convention in Paris, everyone greeted each other with "bonejour."

The hosiery king was wealthy beyond measure, but personality-wise, people just wanted to sock him.

The hosiery king employed the best clothing designers to work on indestructible nylons because he wanted to have a leg up on his competitors.

You can always tell a forestry product specialist by the way they lumber along.

To stay in business, bookbinders have to cover their costs.

Astronomers do it at night under a star-spangled sky and it's heavenly.

Telegraphers do it in long and short dashes and no one has to call the next day.

Arborists do it in the trees because they're young and limber.

Older arborists do it indoors because their limbs aren't up to it.

Obstetricians do it and it's all in the delivery.

Sign language interpreters do it, but they're all hands.

Dentists do it and think they're hot stuff because they're doing the drilling.

Hunters do it and just hope to get a shot in.

Garbage collectors do it but don't always satisfy because of all the trash talk.

Puzzled by a locked door at the hospital, the orthopedic surgeon finally was able to gain access when he found a skeleton key.

The orthopedic surgeon was brought to tears when his son announced that he was going out Trick-or-Treating dressed as a skeleton.

Q: Does every orthopedic surgeon have a skeleton in her/his closet?

A: We'll know only if they come out and say so.

When women orthopedic surgeons came out in favor of equal pay for equal work, they demonstrated they had the spine to take that stand.

When the ladder company became successful, it was necessary to step up production.

When the CEO of the ladder company retired, he had to step down from his position.

In order to stay competitive, the R/D section of the ladder company had to take the right steps.

A firearms manufacturer built a 50-caliber handgun, but after an initial peak in sales, massive numbers of injuries sustained by shooters caused the company to recoil all guns sold.

The egocentric ophthalmologist went to a nude beach and gave everybody an I-full.

Apple designed a smartphone for the egocentric that they've called an I-Phone.

An entrepreneurial optometrist came up with a fashionable pair of glasses for the egocentric: He's calling them designer I-ware.

Some aeronautical engineers approach their work with a wing and a prayer.

Locksmiths work in a key industry.

It is said that because of the FDIC, banking is a safe industry.

The migrant workers disliked weeding the most because each day was a long row to hoe.

On any farm, weeding is an important job. It requires a hoe lot of work.

Q: What's an opportune place to advertise if you're a plastic surgeon?

A: Facebook.

The cardiologist was a true capitalist who specialized in serious heart conditions of the wealthy.

The cardiologist was feeling romantic and murmured sweet nothings to his wife.

Q: Do any orthopedic surgeons have skeletons in their closets?

A: Most likely they do because it represents the body of their work.

At their annual conventions, ornithologists tend to flock together around issues of concern.

When geologists gather together, they refer to earthquakes as "rock and roll."

The owner of the stone quarry stonewalled negotiations in the labor dispute.

Geologists try to be smart when buying a house, wanting to get a house that's dirt-cheap. They examine the location to find solid grounds for underbidding the price.

As skilled civil engineers, beavers love to sink their teeth into a nice dam project.

Once podiatrists have passed their licensing exam, they try their professional best not to be callous in providing services.

In down times, civil engineers sometimes have to put up with a dam project.

The mining company supervisor was told the next major project would be removing the side of the mountain, but it turned out to be a bluff.

Arborists who incorrectly name a species are barking up the wrong tree.

The meteorologist had few friendly colleagues because he was always stealing their thunder.

When the radio talk show host signed off at the end of his daily broadcast, he gave his audience a radio wave.

The argument went on and on because the orthopedist had a bone to pick over everything.

The orthopedist wasn't satisfied with the solution because the issue had long been a bone of contention for him.

The plastic surgeon was a highly skilled specialist but when he made a mistake he just couldn't face the patient.

Radiologists aren't really more highly intuitive or insightful. They can't actually see through you, so don't worry, your secrets are safe.

Carpenters are good at doing it and they call it nailing a project.

Cartographers do it as a way of getting the lay of the land.

Airline pilots do it in the cockpit and refer to it as "bringing her in for a safe landing."

Computer engineers are skilled in doing it because of the high capacity RAM.

The telephone operator-turned-actor was known for her curtain calls.

CHAPTER THREE
THE ARTS

Film photographers do it in a darkroom because they are fascinated by seeing what develops.

Artists, relying on imagery from within, draw upon their inner resources for their artwork.

In the world of art, sculptors have to carve out their niche.

Sculptors don't need drugs to get stoned.

Not all sculptors have chiseled features.

Blacksmiths are very creative artisans working with hammer, metals, and anvil, sometimes they have trouble ironing out specific problems.

Photographers working with lingerie models often have filmsy excuses for why they do it.

You don't want to tick off a professional photographer because he is likely to just snap.

One occupational hazard of blacksmithing is the pounding headaches.

When the sign painter's girlfriend left him for another guy, he was at a loss for words.

If you're a rock star, it's probably not a good idea to live in a glass house.

Jazz musicians do it after a long night of creating music and call it jamming.

Trumpet players do it, but they don't always get the fingering right.

The young artist submitted an art piece in the local art contest and won first prize. He considered it the luck of the draw.

The old music buff preferred to buy vinyl records because he felt they were groovy.

The calligraphy master was in high demand for demonstrations because he was a character himself.

The ballerina's daughter started studying American Sign Language and with her lithe and graceful motions, she learned to sign her name in cursive.

Photographers working on lingerie photo shoots spend extra effort in focusing on the subject at hand.

Q: When the swine artist took up painting, what medium did she choose?

A: Pigment.

Sculptors who were trained by their fathers are usually chips off the old block.

In folk dancing, you have a line dance, a square dance, and a circle dance. Is there a triangle dance, and does it mess up couple's relationships?

An avant-garde New York gallery has a binary art show that has been displayed off and on for a while now.

The company that invented "Paint-by-Numbers" experimented briefly with "Binary Paint-by-Numbers," but its success was hit-and-miss.

A shy introverted artist living in a glass house would likely draw the curtains.

I can see avid photographers living in glass houses. Their whole work centers around exposure.

The artist in the glass house solved the privacy problem simply by drawing the blinds.

If you've ever wondered what classical music you are likely to hear in a cobbler's shop, it would be Shoebert.

Music historians will tell you that the genre with the most up and down history is elevator music.

There's a new book out for artists who perform with marionettes: *Pulling Strings for Dummies*.

An artist's tools are brushes and putty knives, chisels and sanding stones, or cameras and lenses. A writer's tools are his words. That says a lot.

When the silent screen actor retired, there was little fanfare because he was someone you'd never heard of.

After the ventriloquist's dummy delivered the commencement address at the ventriloquist's alma mater, the ventriloquist complimented him and said, "I couldn't have said it any better."

The Hen-House Players were so good, they knew their fowl play was headed for Broadway.

The opera singer was often compared to large church organs because they both have a great set of pipes.

The Wizard of Oz wasn't pleased about the final curtain call.

The Wicked Witch of the East didn't appreciate how her escrow closed.

Standup comedians tend to shy away from using puns in their routines because a lot of people can't stand them and won't sit still for them.

Puns are an acquired taste. They build character, if you can survive the punishment.

The standup comedian felt under a huge pressure to produce because the judge placed him under a gag order.

Four marionette musicians got together and formed a string quartet.

The sculptor received a commission for a large statue in marble and when the huge block arrived, he began chipping away at it a little bit at a time.

Chickens attending the opera found the performance eggsillerating.

The chicken sculptor said the statue eggsemplified truth, beauty, and the American way.

When the chicken symphony conductor was late for practice, her eggcuse was that her cluck was broken.

A mime is always quite comfortable in the library.

The mime's son decided to follow in his father's hand moves.

In their arguments, the mime's wife always had the last hand.

He decided that he wanted to become a mime when he grew up because as a child he was taught he should be seen and not heard.

The symphony board hired a new leader for the symphony who stood only 4 feet tall and introduced him as their semi-conductor.

The veteran chicken actor knew it was more dramatic to eggsit the scene stage left.

When the ventriloquist lost his voice, his partner was at a loss for words too.

Young people find it curious that in their parents' youth, books and information resources in libraries were accessed by the use of a card catalog. What they don't realize is that these were the original digital files.

Comedians who perform at vineyards are looking for a barrel of laughs.

The comedian made jokes at his own expense. He made up for it by claiming it on his expense account.

Some comedians rely on materials from all sources, but choose to stay away from cursing and profanity. It's a principle they swear by.

The comedian in a wheelchair laments that it's been difficult being a standup comedian.

While it has been tough for the comedian in a wheelchair, he tries to roll with the punch lines.

There's a new book out for ventriloquists: *Thought Projection for Dummies*.

Volume II in a series for ventriloquists: *Diction for Dummies*.

Volume III in a series for ventriloquists: *Pronouncing Difficult Words for Dummies*.

Volume IV in a series for ventriloquists: *Speaking Your Mind for Dummies*.

Volume V in a series for ventriloquists: *Projecting Your Voice for Dummies*.

Volume VI in a series for ventriloquists: *Vocabularies for Dummies*.

Volume VII in a series for ventriloquists: *Ventriloquism for Dummies*.

The marionette's cardiologist warned him to change his lifestyle because he was too high-strung.

The ventriloquist was deep in salary negotiations with the director of the film because he said he had two speaking parts.

Assessing participation at a ventriloquist's convention isn't easy because there are always twice as many attendees than people who registered.

The marionette violated work-related rules and was suspended for his infraction.

Marionettes are notoriously gullible. It's so easy to string them along.

Sometimes puppets get a bad rap for being lazy, but in reality, they're highly dedicated and always on hand.

The lion went to the audition because he thought he was perfect for the mane part.

Puppets are generally great at children's parties, but they sometimes can be a handful.

When marionettes party, it's all too easy for them to hang one on.

Broadway directors do it behind the curtains and it's called staging.

When the ventriloquist was given a primetime TV show, it was considered a two-part series.

The judgment against the ventriloquist said that it isn't protected speech just because his dummy said it.

A ventriloquist rarely has to struggle to get a word in edgewise while working with his dummy.

Professional folk dancers go around in the best of circles.

The avant-garde designer of a new line of clothing got into deep trouble because he was all for transparency.

The distinguished clothing designer went to a high-end bar and had a belt or two. His friend also tied one on.

The rabbit weaver is an artist and does his best work on his hareloom.

Hummingbirds are just obnoxious after they've seen a stage musical.

Hummingbirds always seem to remember the score, but the lyrics tend to elude them.

Claude Monet was confident in his innovative approach to painting and gave the impression that he knew exactly what he was doing.

As a sculptor, Michelangelo rocked the art world of his day.

Michelangelo's David is one of the marbles of the Italian Renaissance period.

Michelangelo's father was an artist in his own right, which made little Michelangelo a chip off the old block.

Impressionism emerged during the late 19th century as a new art form and traditionalists couldn't brush off its influence.

The village blacksmith celebrated his 25th wedding anniversary with his wife, but he overdid it and got really hammered. She nailed him for it.

Art critics felt impressionist painters somehow gave the wrong impression.

Claude Monet was a true artist in love with his art. He did it for the love of it and not for the Monet.

CHAPTER FOUR

WORDS AND LANGUAGE

There's a new book out for ventriloquists: *Articulation for Dummies*.

There's a second new book out for ventriloquists: *How to Lip-Sync for Dummies*.

The ventriloquist decided to run for political office and bought the book, *Politics for Dummies*.

Noun and Verb were arrested by the Grammar Police and convicted of colluding in the wrong tense and are now serving a short sentence.

Noun was brought in for questioning by the Grammar Police and is the prime subject of an ongoing investigation.

The Grammar Police felt they had to bring Verb in for questioning because of his actions.

The Grammar Police's investigation was stymied because Noun's accomplice, Verb, was missing, and the sentence they were colluding on was going nowhere.

The Grammar Police arrested Ellipsis for not coming to a full stop at the end of a sentence.

The Grammar Police had to investigate a case of Ellipsis being too lackadaisical in ending a sentence.

When the Grammar Police interrogated Ellipsis, they found him hesitant in ending a sentence.

The Grammar Police are frustrated they can't arrest a semicolon for "stop-and-go" because it isn't against the law.

The Grammar Police were suspicious that Ellipsis wasn't telling everything he knows.

With Ellipsis murdered, the Grammar Police weren't able to find out what he didn't say.

The Grammar Police found that Period came to an abrupt stop at the end of the sentence and was rear-ended.

The Grammar Police stopped Ellipsis for a traffic violation because he made a rolling stop at the end of a sentence.

The Grammar Police will tell you that the excessive use of the comma isn't good for writing, but that is not comma knowledge.

Is it possible for a paraplegic to be a standup comedian?

There's a new play coming to Broadway titled, "The Amazing Technicolor Book of Puns." It's a play on words.

No one likes Apostrophe because he's so possessive.

The Grammar Police were involved in a sting operation and Apostrophe was arrested for possession with intent to sell.

When the Grammar Police assessed the situation of Apostrophe, they called in a priest because it was a case of possession.

Some writers are superstitious enough that they avoid having a Chapter 13 in any of their works.

The Grammar Police stopped Apostrophe on suspicion of possession, but he claimed he just likes to hang with friends.

The Grammar Police broke up the party to arrest Apostrophe, but in reality it was Comma on a high.

Apostrophe and Comma are cousins. When the Grammar Police stop them, the main way to tell them apart is to grab the high one for possession.

Comma is a really smooth character. When he dances with Sentence, he has that pause step that thrills her.

The records of the Grammar Police don't show that Comma has ever been arrested for making an illegal stop.

It takes getting used to Exclamation Mark because he is so loud.

No, you wouldn't say Exclamation Mark was an introvert.

When the Grammar Police found Question Mark in a daze, they asked him what happened, but he hadn't a clue.

The Grammar Police figure Exclamation Mark was on some substance because of his exaggerated emotional state.

The Grammar Police originally thought they had Apostrophe on a possessions charge but it turned out to be a contract violation.

The Grammar Police were called because Clause was in the brackets.

Apostrophe's husband grabbed the overnight bag and drove her to the hospital because of her contractions.

Question Mark was picked up for loitering by the Grammar Police because someone called in a complaint about a questionable person in the neighborhood.

When the Grammar Police brought Question Mark in for questioning, he didn't have any answers.

When Pronoun was being questioned by the Grammar Police, he kept changing the subject.

Pronoun always hated the childhood game of tag because he was always "it."

To the Grammar Homicide Detective, murdering the English language is a major crime requiring capital punishment and a long sentence.

During a news conference regarding abbreviations, The Chief of Grammar Police made a brief comment.

Cursive writing is an ancient and beautiful skill. It doesn't have anything to do with swearing unless you have difficulty doing it.

At some point, a writer has to decide on the morality of plagiarism, whether it's write or wrong.

Is it a peripheral conversation when you can't get a word in edgewise?

If you send an email in all caps, is it considered express mail?

Deadline: The punch line to a really bad joke.

The Grammar Police gave the writer a warning about run-on sentences when he was going through a bad period in his writing.

The Grammar Police had to let the adjective go when he modified his statement.

According to the Grammar Police, an action movie is one predicated on a wild and daring chase sequence.

The verb's explanation to the Grammar Police didn't hold up because they caught him in the act.

Pronoun was held for questioning because he didn't properly identify himself.

The Grammar Police told the distraught comma, "Pause and take a breath, and then go on and tell us what happened."

The Grammar Police were called in on a domestic dispute. Period accused Comma of being indecisive and hesitant. Comma shot back that Period was close-minded and brought everything to a halt. Only one was arrested.

As the Grammar Police approached the feline writer's home, they were warned about her sharp clause.

When Noun and Verb went camping, the Grammar Police were called because the two were sleeping in the wrong tense.

When Noun and Verb received the package from the sporting goods store, they called the Grammar Police because their camping tense didn't match.

Bet you didn't know that ty-ping paper is considered classic Chinese stationery.

My dad was an immigrant to this country and spoke broken English. I wonder how hard it was to break it in.

The Raven is an example of a Poe excuse for literature.

The beat poets specialized in writing poems with no rhyme or reason.

There's a new meaning to the quote: "The pen is mightier than the 'S' word."

As a successful author, he was able to build a fine barbecue pit with all the writer's blocks he'd gathered over the years.

The chicken censors sought to eggspurgate certain sections of the manuscript because they were objectionable.

Puns are a serious threat to visual health. They can cause severe rolling of the eyes.

Grammarians are totally strict about the use of punctuation, period.

One thing that drives grammarians crazy is the overuse of periods. It just has to stop.

It doesn't add to the quality of your writing if you use too many commas so you should pause for a while.

The solution to sentences that don't go anywhere is to adverbs.

Stream-of-consciousness poetry is often unintelligible and stanza part from the rest of literature.

To truly appreciate poetry, one needs to know the word's worth.

English poets fascinated with small trucks are known as poet lorryettes.

Sign language interpreters can raise their voice and yet not be heard.

When Four, For, and Fore met for the first time they learned that they were triplets separated at birth.

Four, For, and Fore were reunited after learning they were triplets separated at birth. They started dating Two, To, and Too, who they met at a support group.

Four, For, and Fore met at a support group for victims of identity theft. They found they had something in common.

The triplets Two, To, and Too, were apprehended operating an identity theft ring. They had similar backgrounds.

The triplets Four, For, and Fore got into frequent trouble as teenagers. Even their Grammar Ann had difficulty telling them apart.

The triplets, Two, To, and Too, worked for years as stunt doubles in the movies. It was hard to tell them apart.

The triplets Two, To, and Too, were named after a distant relative from ancient Rome by the name of Et Tu.

Four, For, and Fore thought they might be related. They said that sounded about right.

When the triplets, Four, For, and Fore, passed the DMV test their driver license photos were hard to tell apart.

Why isn't the word "abbreviate" a shorter word like "shorten?"

Why is the word "long" shorter that the word "short?"

Why are "brief" and "short" longer words than "long," and "shortest" is longer than them all?

Why is the word "shorter" longer than "short?" Is this a conspiracy?

In English, a word is not more impressive for its length. It should be short and sweet, like "chocolate."

That a collection of letters can stand for something is impressive. It definitely says something about language.

Bullies use harsh and brutal words to mean what they say.

Words are the weapon of choice of bullies who prey on the vulnerable; their words are filled with meaning. It is intentional and they mean to do it.

Writers turn to their thesaurus to enrich their story lines. Or, is it enhance?

The novice writer was arrested by the Grammar Police for publishing indecent materials because she used too many dangling participles.

The writer didn't stand a ghost of a chance of finding someone to write his autobiography.

Writers make sense of their stories by using memories of sight, sound, touch, taste, and smell.

To a writer, a thesaurus is an invaluable tool. There's another word for it, though.

A punster, when faced with the punitive punishment of unaccepting pundits, knows that when it's fourth and long, it's best to punt.

The three brothers, Four, For, and Fore, were very different personalities: One you could always count on, one was there for you, and the youngest always had to be first.

The three sisters, Sent, Scent, and Cent, ended up in very different professions: One worked for the Post Office, one trained law enforcement blood hounds, and the youngest wrote puns for money.

The three sisters, Two, To, and Too, were very close: One was a twin, one had direction in her life, and the youngest followed in her middle sister's footsteps.

The three brothers, Eye, Aye, and I, were very ambitious: One studied and became an optometrist, one went into piracy, and the youngest became a politician

The three sisters, Mean, Mine, and Mein, were very different personalities: One didn't play well with others, one was selfish, and the youngest was shallow and superficial.

The three sisters, Merry, Marry, and Marey, were each single-minded: One loved to party, one had to get married, and the youngest loved to horse around.

The three brothers, Poor, Pour, and Pore, fared differently in life: One had a gambling addiction and ended up penniless, one loved his job as a bartender, and one became a dermatologist.

The three cousins, Abode, Aboard, and Abroad, have very different lives: One is a stay-at-home mom, one is a conductor on a commuter line, and the youngest travels extensively for her work.

The Grammar Police arrested Comma and Period for colluding in the creation of multiple run-on sentences.

After Period was convicted, the Grammar Police weren't sure if any laws were broken when he began a sentence.

The Verb actor did a three-week ride-along with the Grammar Police studying for the part of an officer in an action movie.

Sometimes the Grammar Police have quiet stretches when there aren't any problems to speak of.

It used to be tense among the Grammar Police, but that's all in the past.

The Grammar Police wants to ensure the proper use of language because it's the write thing to do.

Improper language use as a write of passage will invariably draw the attention of the Grammar Police.

Foul language isn't a proper write of passage and is sure to catch the attention of the Grammar Police.

Poetic license won't shield you from the Grammar Police, especially if there's no rhyme or reason to it.

If your sentence structures are complex with intertwining clauses, you merely compound the problems for the Grammar Police.

The Grammar Police arrested the ventriloquist's dummy for poor language, but the judge threw the case out because he was just quoting someone else.

The Grammar Police apprehended a gang of clauses who had colluded in the construction of overly complex sentences.

The three sisters, Buy, By, and Bye, fared differently in life: One loved the Shopping Network, one stood with you through everything, and the youngest got ahead without even trying.

There and Their were twins, one of whom grew up not knowing her place, the other resenting always having to share.

The three brothers, Feet, Feat, and Fete, were very close: One was an Olympic 100-meter medalist, one an Olympic long jump champion, and the youngest was an organizer of Olympic ceremonies.

The twin brothers, Faint and Feint, were quite different and enigmatic: One you hardly knew was around, and the younger "floated like a butterfly."

The sign language interpreter worked handily with several languages.

One of the charges of the Grammar Police is to pause the excessive use of the comma.

A radical thought for the Grammar Police to consider putting an end to all sentences, period.

The charge placed on the Grammar Police is to strictly enforce proper use of the English language, period.

The Grammar Police were called in because the guy was in the park exposing his dangling participle.

There is a surgical procedure if you don't know how to use the colon. At the end, you wind up with a semicolon.

It is the job of the Grammar Police to arrest you for improper use of the English language. It is the judge's responsibility to sentence you for a period.

The Grammar Police are sometimes sent to investigate certain comedians because of reports of bad puntuation.

The Grammar Police are frequently called upon to investigate the misuse of "I" and "me" in sentences. As for I, it's not an issue.

In the most serious of infractions, Grammar Detectives are called upon to investigate. In this instance the case was given to I.

Grammar Police are keeping an eye on writers of action novels because they say it's the verbiage that's in question.

Using the same noun twice in a single paragraph will catch the eye of a zealous Grammar Police officer. It's for violating the renouned principle.

For the Grammar Police, nouns are all too often the subjects of their investigations.

The Grammar Police find it is often the case that improper verb tenses are actionable matters.

When the Grammar Police receive a complaint involving verbs, they're ready to swing into action.

The Grammar Police were called to investigate a case of a writer who, during surgery for writer's block, was put into an induced comma.

The Grammar Detective called the paramedics about a case involving a writer. He had a serious case of writer's block that resulted in his being commatose.

The Grammar Police was called to investigate a clown's misuse of commady in front of children.

The Grammar Police were puzzled to learn the writer wrote a story without using any verbs. They found no actionable charge.

The Grammar Police were able to break up the Mafia Language Gang when the capo, Noun, became a subject of interest.

After the trial ended with a conviction, the period's attorney filed a motion to overturn and end his sentence.

Grammar Police are often called upon to reassure English language users by saying, "There, their, they're."

The novice linguist was told an excellent place to study Sanskrit was on the beaches of Hawaii. She found there wasn't a grain of truth in that suggestion.

The ventriloquist and his dummy decided to go home for the holidays, and he packed the dummy in a suitcase. As for the flight, it wasn't much to speak of.

When the ventriloquist was young and just starting his career, he was low on cash so he couldn't advertise his performances much. He had to rely on word-of-mouth.

When the ventriloquist ran for public office his dummy actually won the seat because he was the better speaker.

A ventriloquist's worst nightmare is that his dummy is mute.

A ventriloquist's second worst nightmare is that his dummy becomes a sullen teenager.

A ventriloquist is just one explanation for someone who talks with himself.

When singers lip-sync, is there a ventriloquist back stage somewhere?

The senior translator for the deaf was invited to speak at the Mime University's commencement ceremony, but he declined because he felt he didn't know the signs of the times.

Translators for the deaf have found it impossible to post on any social media platform. They can't even sign the agreement.

The ventriloquist's dummy wrote an autobiography that became a New York Times' bestseller, *Living With Someone Who is Forever Putting Words in Your Mouth*.

Sitting around all day thinking up puns is a tough assignment, but someone has to do it and I can take the punishment.

The pun writer was insulted because some critic impuned his character.

Neuroscientists have identified an area of the brain highly reactive in creators of puns called the "puntic trench." It takes words and scrambles their meanings to elicit a laugh.

The master ASL interpreter was in great demand because he excelled in giving audiences a hand.

The young poet sent poems to his beloved written in beautiful script because he was so font of her.

When the marionette auditioned for the symphony orchestra, it was for the string section.

The dummy of the introverted ventriloquist had little to say about most things.

Q: What would a sign language translator do at a national convention of mimes?

A: Be on hand to translate.

Sign language interpreters have skills you can count on the fingers of both hands.

CHAPTER FIVE

HOBBIES AND SPORTS

You should know that as a hobby, fishing can be enjoyable and reel relaxing.

If you're thinking of beginning an exercise plan, know that yoga can be a real stretch.

Indianapolis speedway drivers travel in fast circles.

Watching a basketball game must be pretty gross, what with all the dribbling on the court.

I'm wondering, why do we call round glass balls marbles and not marballs?

Every marathon runner trains at length to avoid "hitting the wall" during a race; most runners are past the stage where "hitting the streets" is any problem.

The young contractor was sorely disappointed when he didn't qualify for the Olympic fencing team.

The athlete was embarrassed he injured himself; he said he'd been attacked by a dog when he simply barked his shin.

The fishing contest was very close, but the crotchety old fisherman eventually won by angling an advantage.

After his team is penalized for an infraction, does the coach use foul language?

Chinese Olympic boxers developed an ingenious defensive tactic they named the Peking Duck.

The rookie chicken shortstop's professional career ended rather quickly because all he could hit were fowl balls.

Serious mountain climbers have to maintain excellent physical conditioning in order to achieve peak performance.

Hiking cross-country in wilderness areas has its ups and downs.

He wasn't very good at folk dancing. Sometimes he'd just get out of line.

The children's game of musical chairs can be rough. Some will win by deseat.

The program director of a local YMCA initiated an activity for the nerdier population called "square dancing."

You know there's a problem when men tell their wives they're attending church services late at night when they're really at an organized craps game called the "Holy Rollers."

Do you know what music people of Oklahoma love? Karaoke!

The gambler overestimated his chances of winning; in the end, it just wasn't in the cards.

Do dealers in Las Vegas casinos walk with a shuffle?

How high is a stacked deck?

How do you continue playing cards if you cut the deck?

Losing heavily in cards can be stressful. You just have to learn to deal with it.

When the striptease artist began considering her retirement, she thought it might be exciting to pursue a career as a standup comedian because she was always able to titillate an audience.

The striptease artist felt her options in retirement were unlimited because whenever she'd been confronted by obstacles in her life, she'd just bare down.

The striptease artist wasn't a terribly complex person. She lived her life based on the spare and naked truth.

The one life lesson the striptease artist gained from her professional life was that when on stage, you're stripped of all pretense.

Striptease artists feel that severe critics of the art form are just clothes minded.

To achieve prominence as a striptease artist, one must develop the consummate skills of disrobing and have the best of exposures.

A skilled striptease artist has a routine with layers of nuance.

Playing cards just may not suit your personality.

After working for 40 minutes to start a fire in the rain, the scout leader succeeded through a stroke of good luck.

The chicken's eggsercise regimen required that she eggspend aerobic energy thirty minutes five days per week.

The chicken won the biggest pot in Las Vegas history, but he knew enough not to ruffle any features by eggsulting in his winnings.

The chicken race driver always drives his mini cooper and eggscelerates when coming out of a curve.

The chicken race driver was so good, he had everyone eating his eggshaust.

The young man was a real pain in the neck. Women considered him up the crick without a paddle.

The chess champion had a checkered history that kept him one jump ahead of his competition.

Chess and checkers are both played on the same game board, but it's only in chess that all the front-line moves are straightforward.

Chess and checker pieces have very different moves, but it's only in checkers that you can jump to a conclusion.

Chess and checkers both have a royal element, but only checkers lets you have a crowning moment.

Striptease as an art form relies mainly on the delicate removal of one's clothing. Wardrobe costs are thus kept to a bare minimum.

A striptease artist's portfolio is put together to emphasize her primary body of work.

Striptease is an art form that has to do with baring one's soul.

In chess, the Queen's knights make one L-of-a-move at each turn.

The origins of chess have been incorrectly reported. It was not created in India, as commonly thought, but in Australia. How else can you explain the concluding move: "Check, Mate!"

The long-term strategy for both chess and checkers involves capture of pieces, but it is only in checkers that you get the jump on your opponent.

How can I be "out of shape" if I'm the shape I am?

The fisherman planned well for life after retirement with a most interesting bucket list.

The young rodeo star was planning ahead with his bucket list for when he retires.

Younger rodeo stars want to change the face of the sport, but the old-timers are bucking the new trends.

A joker is someone who isn't playing with a full deck.

When the professional athlete had an operation performed by a podiatrist, he had his insurance company foot the bill.

The Olympic long distance runner gave everyone a run for the money.

The Olympic gymnast was so good, she won her floor exercise routine, hands down.

It's been difficult for the boxer in a wheelchair to make it, but he tries to roll with the punches.

The boxer-turned-standup comedian had little trouble mastering his punch lines.

The comedian-turned-boxer couldn't make the transition because he was already way too punchy.

The Olympic gold medalist in cycling was the spokesman for the International Recycling Association.

Bicycle salesmen are known for coming up with creative ways to peddle their wares.

The mallard lost his Golden Gloves bout when his manager yelled, "Duck!" and he thought he was being called.

The Zamboni driver at hockey games ices it every time.

A young man was arrested in the women's bathroom at a Star Trek convention. His excuse was that he was going "where no man has gone before."

Some would question whether striptease is an art form, but as the saying goes, "beauty is in the eye of the beholder," and there are plenty who are beholding.

In the olden days, striptease artists used large fans as part of their routines and patrons or benefactors often came away with a feather in their caps.

When dating a striptease artist, you should avoid bringing up certain topics lest things get touchy.

When a striptease artist goes on a date, what she chooses to wear can be very revealing.

Q: Who was the most powerful dog on the starship Enterprise?

A: Scotty.

The avid kite fan was able to get tickets to the championship kite-flying meet because he got wind of the dates.

What kind of key do you need to open a headlock? I don't know, but you have to wrestle someone for it.

The Olympic gymnast had a lock on the gold medal because of her tumbler routine.

AARRGGH...! You think you have it tough? A pirate's life is so bad, he doesn't have a peg to stand on. You can parrot that around.

The Olympic long-distance runner fell during the 10,000-meter race and injured his leg. "I'm out of shape," he said lamely.

The Olympic high jumper was disqualified because it was found she had a spring in her step.

The Olympic high jumper was banned for a year because of a problem with performance-enhancing substances. She was guilty of oiling the spring in her step.

The ventriloquist had to cancel his Las Vegas show when he got laryngitis. His dummy was at a loss for words.

The young ventriloquist wasn't very good at his craft and decided he'd be better off if his dummy was a silent partner.

The ventriloquist's dummy was thinking about leaving the team because the ventriloquist was always putting words in his mouth and always had the last say.

The ventriloquist's dummy was so angry at his partner, he bought the book: *Passive Aggressive Resistance for Dummies.*

On their days off, rodeo clowns still like to horse around.

Muhammad Ali once received a visit from the Grammar Police because there was a question about his punchuation.

Even NFL players aren't immune from the scrutiny of the Grammar Police. Kickers are often investigated over questionable puntuation, and they know they have to play ball with the police.

People were puzzled because the street corner mime just stood there with his hands in his pockets. They didn't know he was on a jury and the judge placed them under a gag order.

The Olympic pole-vaulter earned his law degree and set an Olympic record the same year, thus passing the bar twice.

When the mime was arrested for breaking and entering, he was handcuffed. When questioned by detectives he was at a loss for words.

During heavy winters, when mimes wear mittens, it's hard to understand them because their conversation is muffled.

When the master clock maker retired, he was glad to relax and wind down.

The ventriloquist picked up a volume of the new book, *Shakespearean English for Dummies.*

The ventriloquist's dummy's job is the harder of the two. He has to follow the ventriloquist's lead based solely on verbal cues.

The ventriloquist's dummy knew something was seriously wrong when he started hearing voices.

Ventriloquism was a big part of the family heritage; for generations, the tradition had been passed by word-of-mouth.

The master samurai sword maker was innovative and on the cutting edge of technology. He was thought to be really sharp in his trade.

The master samurai sword maker was, pound-for-pound, considered the best with a piece of steel, a hammer, and his anvil.

The ventriloquist bought the New York Time's best seller, *I.Q. Tests for Dummies*.

The ventriloquist was puzzled when someone sent him a copy of the book, *Speech Disorders for Dummies*.

Several of my unfit friends have organized the Challenge Olympics: events include leaping to conclusions, begging the question, casting aspersions, catching a cold, running an errand, dashing a hope, passing an opportunity, spotting an error, floating a loan, diving right in, and throwing in the towel.

The young ball player went to spring training tryouts for a professional team and he was surprised when they asked him to pitch his best line.

Mimes sometimes want to branch out and explore other avenues of self-expression. Unfortunately, people tend to put them all in the same box.

The ventriloquist's dummy started writing a memoir but gave it up because he found he didn't have an original thought of his own.

It is well understood that the kind of music golfers prefer is swing.

When the mountain climber's wife caught him in the embrace of a younger woman, he protested she was making a mountain out of a molehill.

Puns definitely are an acquired taste: for some they're filet mignon, for others they're just baloney.

Comedians are smart and know puns are an acquired taste. They still rely on them to help bring in the bread.

You don't normally associate puns with religions, but you will find them in texts dealing with punishment.

The genius marionette was forever getting into trouble with law enforcement because, though not a drug user, he was frequently strung out.

The marionette businessman had some trouble dealing with others because he thought there were strings attached in every transaction.

Manny the ventriloquist wasn't doing well in the business because his dummy trained as a mime.

When they're first getting started in show business, marionettes need to have the right pull.

Marionettes love murder mysteries because they always leave the reader hanging by a thread.

Marionettes are truly safety conscious; they know that so much hangs on their every move.

The marionette businessman had a type-A personality and was highly strung.

Sonny is a very insecure marionette and everyone easily pulls his strings.

Most golfers have a handicap, but it is a pre-existing condition that is not covered under the Affordable Care Act.

Golfers with a handicap are not covered by the Americans with Disabilities Act.

The interesting thing about a ventriloquist's performance is it's considered a solo act.

A marionette and a puppet went out on a date but it turned out to be a disaster because there was no one there to speak for them.

The marionette regretted challenging friends to a game of cat's cradle.

The softball players from the bakery loved the part of the game where they could yell, "Batter up...!"

Skydivers do it at 14,000 feet and just have to watch not to get tangled in their cords.

Mimes do it, but it's nothing to speak of.

Pilots do it, but their relationships are always up in the air.

Rodeo cowboys do it but their partners aren't always pleased with how much they like to horse around.

Baseball players are always trying to do it, but sometimes they only get to second base.

Baseball pitchers think they're hot stuff, but sometimes they pitch a shutout.

Basketball players do it and like to get it in with only net.

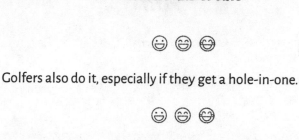

Golfers also do it, especially if they get a hole-in-one.

Pool players do it right on cue.

Bowlers do it in an alley.

Archers do it by keeping a sharp eye on the target.

Hockey players do it by sticking the puck in the net.

Frisbee players do it but it's often just a fling.

Olympic target marksmen do it and are always willing to give it a shot.

Professional cyclists do it because when done well, it's the ride of a lifetime.

Pool players do it by putting balls into pockets.

Long distance runners do it as something they take in stride.

Olympic 100-meter sprinters do it, but it's all over so quickly.

When the timer at the track meet was asked if he was ready, he said, "Just a second."

In the chicken minor leagues, players start out hitting a lot of fowl balls.

When rodeo performers reach a certain age they find for the sake of their health it's wise to retire, but the really good ones are still able to throw the bull around.

The best rodeo cowboys are mavericks. They all relish bucking the system.

If rodeo cowboys stay too long in the profession or become too careless, they often become the subject of "Breaking News."

Dating a striptease artist has got to have a few land mines. Some subjects you can't touch, as she won't want to bare herself.

Popular striptease artists will perform as many shows as the traffic will bare.

With the upswing in pun enthusiasts coming out of the closet, there is a drastic need for public support of common sense pun-control.

In the area of humor puns are an acquired taste, usually made more palatable by your best buds.

Q: What is it called when a Sikh standup comedian pokes fun of you?

A: It's a Pun-jab.

Q: What is it called when a drunken newscaster uses a play-on-words to report the news?

A: They say he's a punditz.

CHAPTER SIX
LAW AND MILITARY

When the President's family picnic was hit by a cold hard rain, the band struck up "Hail to The Chief."

When someone is running for public office they're thoroughly vetted. This is to see if they ever served in the military, and sometimes it's to see how they love and care for their pets.

The two egocentric politicians cut their debate short because they were both me-deep in conversation and neither could get a word in edgewise.

When the Air Force pilot failed to qualify for the space program, he joined the ranks of the astronaughts.

The pilot in the 57th Chicken Fighter Squadron was a victim of friendly fire when he shot himself down by gunning his engine.

Pilots of the 57th Chicken Fighter Squadron loved piloting fighter aircraft because they were in total control in the cockpit.

When the colonel retired from the 57th Chicken Fighter Squadron, he thought he'd start a fast-food franchise in Kentucky.

Pilots of the 57th Chicken Fighter Squadron are a tight group and think of themselves as birds of a feather.

Pilots with the 57th Chicken Fighter Squadron are fiercely modest and getting them to tell about their exploits is like pulling hen's teeth.

The inexperienced officer improperly arrested the Shepherd Academy graduate because he was told the student was in a business with crooks.

The economy was tight during WWII and the pay for pilots of the 57th Chicken Fighter Squadron was so low, they felt they were being paid chickenfeed.

Contemplation isn't a trait you'd normally ascribe to spies, but some have been known to engage in naval gazing.

The chicken detective had a reputation for solving crimes quickly because he could eggstrapolate from scant evidence.

What you didn't know is that the CIA recruits persons with lower IQs for their counter-intelligence division.

When young Owl was appointed to a judgeship, he first served on the Fly-by-Night Court.

Sailors graduating from the U.S. Naval Academy like to slow dance at the reception because it involves a naval engagement.

There are some politicians who should be on the stage performing in "The Lyin' King."

The best-selling lunch served in the congressional dining room is the classic baloney sandwich, with sour grapes for dessert.

It is a proven fact that to anger a judge is to court major troubles.

There are some countries in the world where wars rage, making them unsafe terrortories.

The young ear of corn was considered a rising star in the Marine Corps; he quickly rose to the rank of kernel.

The potato failed the physical for the Army because of his multiple eye troubles.

The potato private went out on the town, got mashed, and ended up in the brig.

It's a mistake to think Army paratroopers aren't a highly disciplined military unit just because they hang around a lot.

The chicken attorney hatched a plan to eggshonorate her client.

When the oppressive regime shut down the newspapers, radio, and TV sources, the nation became depressed.

Do you ever wonder if "artificial intelligence" (AI) has gotten totally out of control? How else do you explain congress?

The chicken navigator aboard a WWII flying fortress had the reputation of never getting lost on her way to a target or getting home because unlike her male counterparts, she always stopped and asked for directions.

Pilots of the 57th Chicken Fighter Squadron are confident enough in their knowledge about flaps that they don't need to wing it.

Chicken pilots flying B-17s during WWII had instinctive knowledge to feather the engine's prop when one of their engines caught fire.

When senior pilots of the 57th Chicken Fighter Squadron retire they are often called dinosaurs, but that's a distinction they bear with honor because it's in their DNA.

I can visualize the meaning of "stand up" but am having a hard time seeing what it means to "stand down."

The candidates gave us such little food for thought that it was hard to stomach this campaign season.

The woman ended her relationship with the judge because she'd expected him to court her.

The elderly judge started dating a younger woman. The jury is still out as to whether it's a good idea or not.

For the king's coronation, the dentist presented him with a gold crown.

The chicken did well giving eggspert testimony for the defense.

The judge ruled that the evidence the chicken provided was eggstraneous to the case.

The chicken senator felt that suggesting the bill about in vitro fertilization was the eggspedient thing to do.

Caught off guard by the reporter's question, the chicken running for office spoke eggstemporaneously.

Chickens running for public office are called upon to eggshibit good common sense.

The chicken detective began with an eggsamination of the clues in the case.

The chicken attorney felt bringing up that issue would only eggsaserbate matters.

Anticipating the county deputy chicken coming to eggspropriate the property, the residents flew the coop.

The chicken judge ruled in an eggsparte decision in favor of the defendant.

No one eggspected the chicken judge to recuse herself from the case.

The chicken was called to testify because of her eggspertise.

Because of her age, the chicken was eggsempt from serving jury duty.

The chicken lawyer objected to the law passed eggs post facto.

The chicken politician trained herself to eggsude confidence during campaign speeches. That's why she's first peck for the position.

Anytime congressional committees meet to consider the budget for the CIA's covert operations, it's always on a hidden agenda.

Congress has no idea the size of the CIA's covert operations budget because of a problem of intentional oversight.

The detective easily solved the train robbery because the suspect had a locomotive.

The Major's presentation at West Point on infantry rifles contained an extensive number of bullet points.

The graduate from the police academy was highly qualified, having earned his third degree.

Crime Scene Investigators are trained in forensick science.

Drug mules occasionally hide drugs in their underwear. DEA agents are wary of reaching in to gather evidence for fear of being pricked.

The chairman of the special senate investigative committee wanted to expose the naked truth about pornography.

The special FBI task force on child pornography didn't want to just handle the problem with kid gloves.

When the police department's task force on illegal pornography released its report to the press, it exposed the widespread extent of the problem.

The special investigative committee was called together to look intensively into illegal pornography. Male senators were especially interested in joining the committee.

The special investigator testifying before a select senate committee on pornography used graphic charts to make his case.

The mathematician joined the Navy's submarine service so he could do subdivision.

Big Bird and Elmo decided they'd go into politics and start a puppet government by setting up offices on a special street in your neighborhood.

Ordinance men working on long-range bombers during WWII stenciled this message on the bombs: "Get a load of this!"

During WWII, allied chicken pilots communicated with each other on their squawk boxes.

In intensive fighting in the air over numerous Pacific islands during WWII, the 57th Chicken Fighter Squadron acquitted itself well and wasn't just a fly-by-night outfit.

During WWII, the enlistments of rookies for the 57th Chicken Fighter Squadron was high, as was the record pace by which they quickly earned their wings.

The pilots of the 57th Chicken Fighter Squadron relished their work because this was the only way they could get off the ground.

Men who flew pursuit planes during WWI wore silk scarves around their necks. That was because they thought they did a dandy job of flying planes.

The Beijing police picked up a man named Thomas accused of being a Peking Tom.

When the largemouth bass was recommended for a federal judgeship, it was with an eye towards affecting the scales of justice.

When screening recruits for the Grammar Police, it's important to ensure the comically unstable don't end up on the streets with a badge and a pun.

The Grammar Police generally avoid getting into politics, but they had to do something when Hyphen said he was a uniter, not a divider.

The Grammar Police surrounded Period with guns drawn and shouted, "Stop right there!"

The Superior Court judge took his daughter to work, where she witnessed a misstrial.

The rooster had a lot to live down as a marine, because when the bullets started to fly around, his buddies said he was a chicken.

The hummingbird specifically joined the Air Force so he could fly helicopters and hovercrafts.

The mallard joined the Air Force and handily earned his wings.

During the severe drought, the self-centered monarch had his royal court perform ceremonial reign dances.

When the furniture manufacturer received a notice from the King's secretary canceling an order for a royal chair, he was thrown for a loss.

When the novice drug runner got wind that the DEA agents were closing in on his transit house, he took a powder.

The Marine Corps company bugler performed in so many ceremonies for fallen comrades that by the end of the day, he was tapped out.

As a unique and consummate conductor and composer, John Phillips Souza marched to his own drummer.

When the toymaker decided to become a dictator, he established a puppet regime.

The dictator was so egocentric, he reigned on his own parade.

The ASL interpreter was in court for the prosecution, where he fingered the suspect.

Sailors with severe hearing deficits don't mind serving on submarines because it's considered the silent service.

When the private failed to carry out the order, the Chicken Colonel told him he was in a peck of trouble.

The Chicken Colonel always thought of the military chain-of-command as a rigorous pecking order.

When the Chicken Speaker of the House closed debate on the measure, the other representatives squawked loudly but to no avail.

Life for the pilots of the 57th Chicken Fighter Squadron was rarely calm. There was always some kind of flap or another.

Chicken bombardiers flying in B-17 flying fortresses during WWII dropped their eggs over enemy oil fields, munitions dumps, and strategic bridges.

The photographer was apprehended by police and charged with an alleged shooting incident. Police were focusing on his motive.

The spirit of brotherhood among pilots of the 57th Chicken Fighter Squadron was strong. In the pitch of battle, they egged each other on.

The first ace among the pilots of the 57th Chicken Fighter Squadron was "Red" from Rhode Island.

Pilots with the 57th Chicken Fighter Squadron were a superstitious lot, always flying on a wing and a prayer.

Did you know that a ship of the Continental Navy under the command of John Paul Jones was named for an orthopedic surgeon? She was the Bonehomme Richard.

The entrepreneurial chicken attorney specialized in cases where clients were afowl of the law.

CHAPTER SEVEN
FOOD AND DRINK

During the annual roundup rodeo, cattle ranchers bet heavily on their favorite bulls because they all have a steak in the winner.

During the prohibition era, the mob branched into areas other than liquor, including high-end barbershops known as clip joints.

Charlie loved working at the chocolate factory, especially because he was sweet on a coworker.

When times are tough at the butter factory, dedicated workers will churn in their sleep.

Is a peach cobbler someone who makes fine shoes out of fruit? Does he make slippers out of bananas?

When the coffee magnate's son left the family business to start his own company, he left with nothing more than a hill of beans.

When the CEO of a coffee company retired, he was concerned he would become nothing but a has-bean.

The orthopedic surgeon was so knowledgeable in his specialty, he easily managed the deboning of the Thanksgiving Turkey.

The foreman at the pepper factory was a seasoned veteran of the business.

The new apprentice to the master baker had a bit of a temper. His colleagues tagged him "Yeast" because it didn't take much to get a rise out of him.

The young butcher was hired to manage the meat department of the grocery chain and was willing to steak his reputation on doing well.

The young man interviewed for the position of butcher and came out a cut above other applicants.

The butcher was quick and efficient in his work and finished all special orders chop-chop.

The butcher took great offense when a customer complained of inferior quality meats. He retorted, "That's just baloney!"

Here's a question for you: Why are shrimp boats so large?

After a full course Chinese dinner, your appetite just might dim sum.

Count Dracula spent his whole life on a diet of fast foods and died sadly with a steak through his heart.

During the Lenten season, there isn't anything you'd call fast food.

Cannibalism: The practice of serving your fellow man.

Matzah: Traditional bread that doesn't rise to the occasion.

At a nudist potluck dinner, are all salads without dressing?

You'll find nothing but sour grapes in whine country.

The chicken was feeling peckish when she ordered a burrito, so she asked for eggstra sauce.

Indian foods are growing in popularity because seasonings are used to curry the favor of diners.

Puns clearly are an acquired taste, so if you have something negative to say about, spit it out.

The new Indian restaurant did well from its opening because the head chef knew that curry flavor would curry favor.

Saw a sign next to the door of a Mexican restaurant that read: "Si you later."

The master Chinese chef was so good, he had the reputation of a wok star.

The fancy Chinese restaurant was known for its excellent wok and roll.

The new breakfast restaurant did so well, the cook staff had to scramble to keep up with the orders.

When the young couple took over management of the successful surf-n-turf restaurant, they had a steak in its success.

The employees of the new burger joint had a beef with the new owners and went on strike.

When the newspaper food critic visited the seafood restaurant, the owners weren't averse to fishing for a good review.

Through hard work, the young Japanese couple was able to rice to the challenge of owning a sushi restaurant.

Puns are an acquired taste, but some comedians are rather insensitive to their audiences and pepper their routines with them.

It is an accepted tenet that puns are an acquired taste. Rarely do you find one to serve as food for thought.

Brewing a great cup of coffee filters down to just a couple of key steps.

The secret to brewing a great cup of tea is sometimes steeped in ancient family traditions.

The wide variety of teas is enough to leaf you impressed and amazed.

Laying eggs is something chickens eggscell at.

Is it improper to serve beer and wine on the coffee table?

The peanut butter sandwich complained to his lawyer that he was caught in a jam.

The peanut butter sandwich got together with a friend for a jam session.

With winter coming on, all the furry critters were furiously squirreling away a supply of nuts.

The peanut butter sandwich was jammed up by someone he thought was a friend.

To produce the best culture for cheese, you have to find the best whey to do it.

The coffee magnate was angered that his bride contested the prenuptial, and considered it grounds for divorce.

The chicken received the "Egg Layer of the Month" award for her eggspeditious use of time. Her secret? She paid close attention to the cuckoo-cluck.

The seasoned baker was famous for his multi-grain breads but when he tried a new recipe, something went arye.

The buzzard family reunion is held annually on the Fourth of July weekend and food is usually potluck. Someone always brings road kill.

Puns are an art form that is an acquired taste. For some they aren't the main course; they're dessert.

The wheat farmer's son was left out of the will because he was caught sowing wild oats.

The baker's daughter surprised her parents when she announced she had a bun in the oven.

The baker's daughter was embarrassed when her boyfriend was caught kneading her dough.

The other day I cut myself while dicing carrots. Mama warned me about being a cut-up.

Small independent coffee shops have a tough time against the mega-corporate shops, but they add a homey flavor to their neighborhoods that the big ones can't.

When the western-themed restaurant decided to move into a larger space, it was easy enough to pick up steaks for the move.

Q: How does a vampire lose weight?

A: He goes on a liquid diet.

Q: How do vampires like their stakes?

A: Rare.

Q: What's a vampire's favorite drink?

A: A Bloody Mary.

Dining on pig's knuckles wouldn't be considered eating high on the hog.

The butcher's son graduated with honors from the Butcher Academy and opened his own shop, knowing full well the steaks were high whether he would succeed.

The jolly butcher was not only an expert on the various cuts of all animals, he was well liked by his customers because it was easy for him to meat the public.

One of the areas the butcher excelled in was healthy preparation of various cuts of meat where he would always lean in the right direction.

The butcher had traveled extensively to many exotic places in the world and loved to share that slice of life with his customers.

In an effort to promote his overall business, the master butcher set up a blog site advertising his special sausages and gave out links to all his customers.

Local police arrested the unscrupulous butcher who attempted to sell "virtual sausages" as part of a weight-loss scheme.

When it comes to humor, puns are an acquired taste that don't appear on all menus.

Puns are an acquired taste and for some, they are definitely hard to swallow.

Here's a puzzle for you: Why is it so easy to pig out on bacon?

Is it still called pigging out if cows do it?

While not the most popular of foods, beets, turnips, and rutabagas can form the roots of a healthy diet.

Q: What do buzzards call road-kill?

A: Dinner.

The new quota for egg production was so high, the chickens found it eggsasperating.

Woodpeckers rely on luck when it comes to finding food—knock on wood.

Beavers always have to watch their diet because they have that continuing gnawing feeling.

The geometry teacher started a new pizza business based on the mathematical pizzapi.

One evening, the jazz pianist brought a jar of peanut butter to a jam session.

The semi-pro ball players from the bakery were in it for the fun, not for the dough.

The mascot for the Little League team was the Idaho Carrot and it didn't take anything to get parents to come out and root for the hometown team.

Don't be surprised the next time you walk into a Chinese restaurant to hear them playing Wok and Roll as background music.

When vampires dine out at a stake house, they order their meals extra rare.

When the old village butcher immigrated to the US and settled in New Jersey, the local detectives suspected he had links to the Mafia.

In terms of one's height, how tall is a short-order cook?

The enterprising entrepreneur had an idea that didn't work out well: A line of fast foods for the religious period of Lent.

The owner of the little pepper factory always sends out season's greetings for the holidays.

Dishwasher: Husbands, when appliances break down.

The seasoning company was celebrating its success because the economy was strong; it truly was the best of thymes.

The seasoning company's security guard was fired because he peppered his language with curse words and customers complained.

The seasoning company's new security guard was ex-navy and his language was pretty salty.

The baker's apprentice was on the job for only three weeks and had to be released because he was caught loafing on the job.

Wine connoisseurs are always looking for a barrel of fun.

Seems to me donut holes are a scientific marvel because they're something made out of nothing.

Unleavened bread is a batch that comes out of the oven after the untenned bread and before the untwelved bread.

😃 😄 😆

Pi: Dessert treats for meetings in mathematical circles.

😃 😄 😆

Can someone translate for me? Is a "latte grande" a tall order?

CHAPTER EIGHT

ANIMALS AND NATURE

To stay connected socially, do snails use shell phones?

Someone needs to create a pesticide specifically for all those things that bug you.

The young and inexperienced rancher called the veterinarian because someone told him that the newborn pony was a little horse.

The eagle didn't mind growing older, because he felt he became more distinguished as he became bald.

In order to tuna fish, you have to start with the scales.

Q: What do you call a seagull that's easily fooled?

A: Gullible.

Horse whisperers work their wonders because their voices are a little hoarse. They work even when they have a little colt.

The thought that feathered dinosaurs were ancestors of present day avians is a theory for the birds.

Recent discoveries indicate that virtually all species of dinosaurs were cold-blooded killers.

The giraffe and elephant were neck and neck throughout the race, but coming down the home stretch, the elephant nosed out the win.

No-Fly-Zone: An enclosed patio space perfect for insect-free parties.

Archaeopteryx was the first dinosoar to fly.

Of all the birds who entered the contest to determine who could fly the highest, the seagull was the soar loser.

Dinosoars are thought to be ancestral to birds for a reason.

After the annual high altitude race everyone's wing muscles were tired, but the seagull was the worst soar loser.

Have you ever wondered if chickens use fowl language?

Archaeologists have discovered fossil bones of a new species of fierce flying dinosoar they've named Pterrordactyl.

When the rooster crows so early in the morning, do the hens wake up in a fowl mood?

The duck was the first in her family to graduate from medical school and her parents were so proud when she hung her shingle as the first medical quack in town.

You would think migrating geese would find it easier to fly when the weather turns fowl.

Are all arborists interested in their own family trees?

If a cow ever became a witch, would she be burned at the steak?

I think I know why a tree's leaves turn red in the fall. They're embarrassed their limbs are going to be buck-naked soon.

The first thing a beaver learns in a computer class is how to log in.

In considering the construction skills of beavers in the animal kingdom, they are a dam site better than all others.

When beavers construct a dam, they always make sure they have food nearby to stave off that gnawing feeling.

After the accident, the owl was in a coma for a while. When she came to, she didn't remember "who" she was.

Owls have special wing feathers that muffle their passage through the air. They are the true stealth fliers.

When the turtle CEO of the company travels on business, he says he doesn't need a housing allowance.

When turtles go into business, do they always start out as a shell corporation?

At the first annual fundraising marathon, the tortoise won by a hare.

When the turtle was in an accident, he was laid up for a time. His recovery was lengthy and he came out a shell of his former self.

The joke, "How do porcupines make love?" is an old one. But what's the point?

The conservation group decided to re-seed the fire-ravaged hillside with young trees to spruce up the place.

The logging company rejected the conservation group's recommendation to stop clear-cutting with the reply, "What fir?"

The vision of an eagle is so sharp, it's been called "sight for soar eyes."

The young man selected to be valedictorian at Shepherd School declined because he was so sheepish.

Shepherd School students wool always be there for ewe.

Shepherd School students learn how to maintain discipline with their flocks by keeping the rambunctious ones in line.

Shepherd School students study hard to avoid being caught up the crook without a paddle.

Learning universal principles in livestock management, Shepherd School graduates take with them the sheep herd around the world.

Chickens are actually highly trained eggsperts.

Personality-wise, the chicken was eggsasperating.

The chickens were advised not to use the emergency procedures except under eggstreme circumstances.

Ineggsperienced pot-smoking chickens have to learn how to eggshale.

Chicken farmers are quick to remind customers to mind the eggspiration dates on the egg cartons.

Sometimes a coroner chicken may be asked to eggshume the body of the deceased.

After a high-production day, chickens are often eggshausted.

The eggsplorer chicken was praised for her leadership with the polar eggspedition.

In order to maintain good health, the chicken started a program of strenuous eggsercise.

Chicken introverts have a hard time eggspressing themselves in public. They tend to lay low.

After the argument, the chicken eggstended her wing as a gesture of reconciliation.

When the rooster came into the yard, the hens were pretty eggscited.

When the chicken came across the problem, she managed it to the eggstent she could.

The chicken team leader took the time to eggstoll the progress everyone made.

The chicken paleontologist believes a gigantic meteor strike was what caused the mass eggstinction of bird-like dinosaurs.

The chicken robber eggsclaimed she was innocent, but the detectives knew she would crack.

The chicken psychiatrist finally convinced her patient that the imaginary demon didn't eggsist; he could finally see the world as sunny side up.

When great grandfather Rabbit died, he left the family hareloom pocket watch to the eldest grandchild.

The rabbit barber was a highly skilled hare specialist.

Baby rabbits can be a hare-raising experience to new parents.

The ram stand-up comedian was booed off the stage because his jokes were so baaa'd. No, they just weren't punny.

When the gang of mollusks was apprehended, their lawyer advised them to clam up until he had a chance to advise them.

The doctor couldn't say what was going on with the mollusk because the only symptom was mussel pain.

Cats have a glorious and legendary history as gods in ancient Egypt. Their descendants won't let us forget it.

Coming from a long history as gods in ancient Egypt, cats have evolved with a sense of entitlement and meow they think they own the place.

When the wolves held their first family reunion, everyone agreed it was a howling success.

When the beaver needed dental work, he got his replacement buckteeth at the dollar store.

The old beaver had let his dental hygiene go for so long, it had finally started gnawing at him.

Beavers concerned with cosmetic appearances can't really do anything with their major overbite.

For the longest time, insurance coverage for beavers didn't include dental. That bites!

Beavers spend a portion of their time beautifying their pond because they want to make their dam site better.

The polar bear made a convincing argument for climate change because of her judicious use of floe charts.

In the forestry industry, lumberjacks dance to logarithms.

The raptor decided he wanted to become a salesman because he felt he'd be good at hawking wares.

After recovering from flying into a high power line, the buzzard took on the nickname "Buzz."

Owls usually have a fly-by-night hunting routine.

With that mischievous smile, you know that Peregrine Falcon is up to no good.

When raptors start dabbling in investments, you know vulture capitalists won't be far behind.

It's a little-known fact that sage hens are as wise as owls.

The mockingbird didn't have many friends because of the way he treated everyone.

Crows often don't do well socially because they're always bragging.

After very humble beginnings, the red bird rose to cardinal in the Catholic Church.

Most birds use social media and know how to tweet.

Sometimes parrots act like mockingbirds. At least that's what they say.

It is a known fact that quails are fraidy cats.

This one Bobwhite prefers you call him Robertwhite until he gets to know you.

Hummingbird mothers are overly protective of their young. They tend to hover.

A flicker is the only North American bird species that will flick you the bird.

The woodpecker is the only bird that suffers headaches just getting a meal.

When they get their nose out of joint, woodpeckers have a hard time getting dinner.

Woodpeckers are fussy eaters. They eat one peck at a time.

Penguins are such party animals. They're always dressed and ready to go at the drop of a top hat.

You rarely see penguins in handsome lead roles, they always end up as the butler.

The roadrunner is a cousin of the cuckoo. Crazy, huh?

Roadrunner is the top salesman of the Acme Explosives Company because he runs circles around everyone.

The sand hill crane got his contractor's license and started his own construction business.

The sage grouse was fastidious and complained about most everything.

It is a little known fact that a seagull's literary collection contains only one volume: "Gulliver's Travels."

The boobie is an awkward bird and there is some flap over how it takes off and lands.

When roadrunners go on a trip, they generally take to the roads.

When looking for a job, canaries avoid any openings in coal mines.

Penguins are an uptight, proper type. You'll never catch one dressed casually, especially at the beach.

Q: Among arborists, which tree is the favorite?

A: The poplar.

There is an ongoing controversy over which came first, the chicken or the egg. Word of advice: avoid the hard boiled advocates on either side.

The conundrum of the chicken and the egg appears to be unsolvable. We may just have to let it lay.

The solution to the question of which came first, the chicken or the egg, may just have to wait for some creative mind to hatch the solution.

The chicken and egg conundrum seems unsolvable. It if comes to a wager, don't put all your eggs in one basket.

A witness observed a feline writer working on her laptop on the beach and reported her to the Grammar Police for sandy clause in the middle of July.

When Pelican placed her groceries on the checkout stand, the checkout attendant asked, "Paper or plastic?" She answered, "Oh, never mind. I brought my own pouch."

The opinionated cattle rancher was known for not taking any bull from anyone.

Fox was disappointed that Turtle didn't come to his defense, but Turtle was afraid to stick his neck out.

The Owl Detective Agency specializes in cases of whoodunit.

It is a well-known fact that lions take great pride in their extended families.

As Thanksgiving approached, the leader of the band of turkeys took charge and said, "Let's get the flock out of here!"

Arborists have an easy time researching their own family trees and relish their findings. They don't pine over the good ole days and can leaf behind the unimportant stuff.

Whenever the beaver colony moved to a new area of the pond, the head beaver's son always brought up the tail.

The young and handsome mollusk actor worked out and was proud of his finely chiseled mussels.

Ornithology students taking their final exams know better than to try and wing it.

Donald Duck worked hard and completed his medical studies, but wasn't granted his medical license because they said he was a quack.

Beaver needed some dental work to replace his front teeth and instead of a porcelain bridge, he thought he'd buck the trend and go with gold.

A young beaver went out with the group to a local bar and happened to meet a toothsome female.

The bats in the belfry learned soon enough it was a crazy idea to build their homes there.

Beavers that become vampires have a difficult time because instead of puncture wounds, they inflict blunt force trauma.

Beavers lead a mostly leisurely life around the pond but sometimes they seem not to give a dam.

Did you know that a favorite nickname for a vampire's pet wolf is "Fang?"

The senior landscape designer had long worked in the area but had the reputation of being a hack gardener.

The landscape gardening profession is rooted in a highly skilled tradition.

The mallard was struck and sustained a concussion when someone shouted, "Duck!" and he turned and waved.

When your friend decides to undertake farming carrots, turnips, and radishes, you just have to root for him to succeed.

The Mollusk family business had been in operation for many generations, but no one knew what exactly they did because it was a shell corporation.

The graduate of the Shepherd Academy showed poor judgment when he arrived at the Halloween party dressed in wolves clothing.

The graduate student at the Shepherd Academy received poor marks in the section on identifying predators because he frequently was caught woolgathering.

If you hear barking out in the woods, what's the likelihood it's a dogwood tree?

The graduate of the Shepherd Academy was so subtle, people didn't realize he was pulling the wool over their eyes.

When the shepherd was asked if he knew about the recent spate of sheep rustlings he answered, "Yeah, I herd."

When the tipsy chicken started swearing like a drunken sailor, the bartender told her she had to stop with the fowl mouth.

The chicken celebrity took advantage of her fame and came out with a line of perfume designed to mask fowl body odors.

When chickens get caught in a rainstorm they get soaked, their feathers get ruffled, and they give off a fowl smell.

Chickens who are raised properly grow up showing clear respeck for their elders and for each other.

The alligator was nicely decked out, wearing his own shoes.

The tuna went to the wedding of his best friend dressed in a sharkskin suit and was roundly criticized by his family.

When the turtle traveled to the site of the Olympics, he had no trouble with housing.

The beaver felt lucky to get the job as head engineer on the construction of the new dam site, but appreciated more that his dental care wouldn't take a big bite out of his earnings.

The beaver had perfect teeth, but only because he had braces as a child.

The beaver tried to avoid smiling and exposing his teeth because he had a terrible overbite.

You would never know it by looking, but beaver has two porcelain crowns in front.

Beavers are forever biting things out of an urge that gnaws at them.

CHAPTER NINE

HISTORY AND MYTHOLOGY

Do you have to turn your sundial back an hour when daylight savings ends?

If a sundial uses Roman numerals, is it giving the time in Rome?

Some of the ritual meanings of the sundial in ancient ceremonies are lost in the shadows of time.

Sundials don't work at all after the sun goes down; that's the dark part of its history.

When you're telling time with a sundial, there's always a shadow of a doubt as to its accuracy.

To discern the mind of an archaeologist, you don't have to dig very deep.

What accounted for the spread of the early Roman Empire? Was it because of the Roamin' Legions?

The mortician and the archaeologist have a very strange kind of relationship: they dig up dates for each other.

The Prodigal Son caused quite a stir at Thanksgiving when he brought a salad to the gathering undressed.

American Indians were the original people who lived in the land of the brave, home of the free. This was before illegal immigrants started coming.

Johannes Gutenberg was a patient man with his first effort because he wasn't pressed for time.

Johannes Gutenberg, inventor of the printing press, left an imprint on the pages of history.

For all the interesting things in their lives, the Wright Brothers led a plane existence.

Thomas A. Edison invented the light bulb, much to the delight of everyone.

It is said Demosthenes placed pebbles in his mouth and shouted against the waves to overcome stuttering. It is also said he had a gravelly voice.

Let's just set the record straight: Thomas A. Edison did invent the phonograph.

David was able to vanquish Goliath by getting into the sling of things.

The origin of puns dates back to the time *Homo sapiens* first stepped out onto the open savanna and exclaimed, "Now that's just plain beautiful!"

Deciphering the language of the Neanderthal is virtually impossible, but those working on it are putting in a lot of grunt work.

In old colonial Williamsburg, the saddest person of all was the town crier.

When archaeologists are working a dig, they have a lot of time on their hands.

Johannes Gutenberg worked slowly to ensure accuracy, and when work piled up, he pressed on.

Johannes Gutenberg did well in the printing business because he was the right type for the job.

Hermann Rorschach failed his own projective testing protocol, which ended up a blot on his reputation.

Henry Ford's engineers came up with a design that fit his model car to a "T."

Young Chicken Arthur drew the sword Eggscaliber out of the stone and beakcame king over the realm.

Zeus reigned as the King of Rain and reined in his subjects with the threat of a thunderbolt.

It's a little known fact that Will Rogers was the first cowboy poet lariat in America.

As a youth, Nicholas II of Russia aspired to be a geologist so he could be a rock tsar.

Early humans learned to count by using their fingers. This was the first digital computer.

There was a time in our past when it wasn't right to be left-handed. It was often handled with a ruler.

Some people thought that being left-handed was a sinister thing. For the most part, we've left that thinking behind.

Icarus made the serious mistake of flying high.

Albert Einstein came up with the one bright formula that really matters.

Werner Heisenberg's colleagues just wished to hell he'd just make up his mind.

Werner Heisenberg almost didn't get married; he just wasn't certain.

Cyclops was one mythological Greek giant with singular vision.

Werner Heisenberg just messed with everybody's minds. He just didn't know.

There were some days Werner Heisenberg didn't know if he was coming or going.

For Werner Heisenberg, there were days when everything seemed to be up in the air.

After his major discovery, Werner Heisenberg wasn't sure of much of anything.

Werner Heisenberg was absolute in his uncertainty. He just didn't know

In Werner Heisenberg's experimental findings, it either was or it wasn't. He couldn't make up his mind.

In exasperation, Werner Heisenberg finally just guessed, because he had a 50% chance he was right.

Werner Heisenberg's first girlfriend rejected his principle because she wanted a lasting relationship.

Neptune's daughter grew up learning to get into the swim of things.

Neptune's daughter had a strict curfew: She had to be home by high tide.

Archaeologists spend most of their time digging around in our past.

Samuel Morse developed a code that enabled him to dash off a message on the dot.

Archaeologists tend to remain apolitical to ensure they don't jeopardize various potential funding sources. Occasionally, one will open his mouth and dig himself into a hole.

Samson wasn't really preoccupied with fashion styles, but he made a statement when he brought down the house over his hair.

Atlas struggled with bouts of depression because he always felt he had the weight of the world on his shoulders.

The anthropologist was only slightly surprised to learn that the young native men tried to scare young native women to get them to jump out of their skins.

In terms of choice in music archaeologists tend to prefer the "golden oldies."

When the Greek owner of an auto towing company suddenly died, his son took over the business and ran it with his mother. They named the new business Oedipus Wrecks.

In the 1950s and '60s, the Burma Shave Company posted roadside sign language for deaf motorists.

When Alexander Graham Bell was working on the first telephone, his contemporary colleagues thought of him as a ding-a-ling.

Early humans witnessed solar eclipses and we know this because someone posted it on the wall of a cave. It isn't clear whether they understood what was happening or if there was a shadow of a doubt.

Preparing for war in ancient times was arduous business, especially for those sharpening swords and spear points, for whom it was a daily grind.

Homer and Jethro's families had been feuding for generations, so when Homer fired 100 rounds into Jethro's house, Jethro sued him for rifling his abode.

Paleontologists spend years researching the origins and early history of the human species. To do this, they have to bone up on volumes of data.

The Emperor Nero was reputed to be a man of low moral character. It is said he fiddled around as Rome burned.

George Washington Carver was a botanist and inventor and was able to make a nice living on just peanuts.

The pioneers of flight learned that certain principles applied to the success of their efforts and knowing this was uplifting.

The Wright brothers had a bicycle repair business and worked hard to get their new interest of powered flight off the ground.

The Wright brothers ran a bicycle repair and manufacturing shop. They decided to establish it as a chain store, but it didn't catch on because they didn't have many links.

Orville and Wilbur Wright were so successful in their efforts in early powered flight that interest in airplanes literally took off.

As bicycle repair specialists, Orville and Wilbur Wright didn't wait long after their successful flight to pedal the idea of airplanes.

Orville and Wilbur Wright got off to a flying start with their attempts at early powered flight.

Orville and Wilbur Wright were successful in their attempts with powered flight because of their plane persistence.

Orville and Wilbur Wright were avid students of manned flight and through extensive study and persistence were not to be foiled.

The Wright brothers were inventors and knew enough from experience that with powered flight, you could not succeed by simply winging it.

When it came to aeronautical design, the Wright brothers relied on plane old geometry.

Orville and Wilbur Wright were interviewed extensively on the local radio station after their successful powered flight. They appreciated the airtime.

The first powered flight by Orville and Wilbur Wright didn't last long. It felt as though the experience just flew by.

When Orville and Wilbur Wright met frustrating situations, they tended to fly off the handle.

When the Chaos Gang attempted to rob a gold shipment on a Union Pacific train, they were so disorganized that their plans were held up.

When actor Pat Morita of *The Karate Kid* movies retired, he started a car detailing business he called "Wax on. Wax off."

When Johannes Gutenberg was a young man, he was pursued by a beautiful young woman who fancied him, but he rejected her because she wasn't his type.

Were stonemasons the originators of the Masonic Order?

When Jesus threw the moneychangers out of the Temple, they were upset because they said they were there for the prophet.

Orville and Wilbur stubbornly pursued their dreams of powered flight and were successful because they made a series of Wright decisions.

Albert Einstein was highly involved with his family but to him, it sometimes was just relative.

It is a little understood fact that J.R.R. Tolkien wrote about vampires in his trilogy, *The Lord of the Rings*, when he wrote about Fangorn Forest.

It is a little known fact of history that vampires were instrumental in the battle of Bloody Ridge in the Korean War.

Archaeologists learn one lesson early in their careers, that being when you dig yourself into a hole, you stop digging.

Cyclops was the go-to guy when it came to negotiating with the enemy because he could always see eye-to-eye with anyone.

Is Mt. Rushmore considered a monument dedicated to a rock group?

Icarus was a bold but foolish son who disregarded his father's warning and made an ash of himself flying too close to the sun.

The archaeologist wondered why the sphinx was placed near the pyramids of Giza, but he ran into a wall of stone in the matter.

The cat was a highly regarded and revered part of the mythology and ideology of ancient Egypt. Some researchers believe it was because early Pharaohs were just feline fine.

It was recorded in several ancient texts that the Pharaoh of the Middle Dynasty wrote about why the pyramid complex at Giza was built in that spot. The sphinx has been silent on the subject.

Were the Pharaohs of ancient Egypt the originators of the pyramid schemes?

The ancient calculator called the abacus lets you get a bead on the correct mathematical answer.

The ancient abacus is a reliable calculating device, one you can count on.

The ancient abacus is a digital calculating device activated by the touch of a finger.

Q: Which Roman god had the most children?

A: Hercules. They were the result of 12 labors.

😀 😁 😄

Q: Who was the most obnoxious and irritating Roman goddess?

A: Aurora. She was an early morning person.

😀 😁 😄

Q: Which Roman god was the life of any party?

A: Bacchus. He always brought the wine.

😀 😁 😄

Q: What Greek goddess actually had her origins in the continent of Africa?

A: Afrodite.

😀 😁 😄

Q: Which Roman goddess is the deity of deli sandwiches?

A: Bellona.

😀 😁 😄

Q: What was the nickname of the Roman god Vulcan?

A: Spock.

😃 😄 😆

Q: Which Roman goddess represents those with injuries and infirmities?

A: Lympha. She walks kind of funny.

😃 😄 😆

Q: Which of the Roman gods was never elevated to deity of transportation?

A: Omnibus.

😃 😄 😆

Q: Which Greek god was known for his speed?

A: Nike. In all competitions, he was shoe-in as winner.

😃 😄 😆

Archaeologists do it because they dig it.

😃 😄 😆

Q: What is the key to "The Theory of Everything?"

A: According to God, it's "Because I said so..."

😃 😄 😆

In its day, *Dante's Inferno* was one hell of an epic poem.

😃 😄 😆

When the operator of the town's sundial was asked if he was ready to monitor the device he said, "Without a shadow of a doubt."

Q: How do vampires check out the branches of their family tree?

A: They check their bloodlines.

Q: When vampires drive around town, how do they get from one place to another?

A: They take the main arteries.

Q: How are vampires like gold miners?

A: They both look for rich veins.

Q: Why is art an attractive profession for vampires?

A: It gives them ample opportunities to draw blood.

Q: What is the attraction for vampires to live in Sierra Leone?

A: It has to do with the blood diamonds.

Q: What is the attraction for vampires of lunar eclipses?

A: They're particularly fascinated during the stage of the blood moon.

There is scant record in our ancient history of solar eclipses. Aside from a few charcoal sketches on cave walls, these events have been lost in the shadows of the past.

Ivan Pavlov lectured widely on his experiments in conditioning, but for some the concept was too esoteric and didn't ring a bell.

In the Old West, blacksmiths were the ones shoeing horses. If their shop was too near the corrals, they were also shooing flies.

Cleopatra was a strong-willed woman and that's not a bad thing, but when she found an asp nearby she shouldn't have said, "Bite me!"

Tourists visiting a Buddhist shrine in San Francisco found a hand-written sign, "No thyself..." ~ Buddha.

Marcel Marceau wanted to team up with someone to start a business but couldn't find anyone who was willing to have a silent partner.

Johannes Gutenberg's work was distinctive; he left his imprint on the publishing world.

Chicken Sartre and Chicken Kierkegaard were both eggsistential philosophers.

Quote: "............!" ~ Marcel Marceau

Do vampires have adequate healthcare that includes dental?

When vampires suffer from a bad colds, they often are bothered with a coffin spell.

The vampire upgraded his computer storage to hold a full terabite.

Vampire surfers can only surf after sundown, and it requires special skills to be board certified.

Most vampires retire when they become senior citizens because dentures typically don't come with fangs.

An increasing problem for aging vampires is they forget why they're nuzzling the neck of a beautiful woman.

One of Shakespeare's mentors recognized the genius of his work and encouraged him on with "May the farce be with you."

Archaeopteryx, the great-great-great-great-great-great-great ancestor of the chicken, went eggstinct a long time ago.

CHAPTER TEN
MATH AND SCIENCE

The astronomer couldn't figure out how to tell time with a sundial after sundown, but it finally dawned on him.

When someone drops their pants and sticks their rear end out, we call it "mooning." Why don't we call it "Uranusing?"

When the cowboy-turned-astronaut went into space and it became utterly dark, he turned on the saddlelights.

To explain the dramatic changes in the Arctic environment, climate scientists rely on the use of floe charts.

The forensic scientist worked ever so hard, but he was eventually let go because he was so clueless.

Climate scientists are not too popular among a certain population because they tend to rain on people's parades.

Climate change is difficult for some people to accept because they feel they're getting a snow job.

A group of hackers broke into a company's computers and stole some binary files. They were caught and the case against them was open-and-shut.

The science of climate change has raised a storm of controversies. The discussions are filled with thunder and lightning.

The eccentric physicist designed a grandfather clock built on a Saturn rocket booster because he wanted to see time fly.

The brilliant scientist invented a 24-hour binary sundial that puzzled the scientific community until someone figured out that he was messing with their minds. The binary device simply was "on" during daylight hours and "off" when the sun went down.

Scientists have created a GPS activated sundial that works after sundown. It tells you where to hold the flashlight.

Earthquake scientists didn't feel they were on shaky ground with their dire predictions.

Because the last major quake occurred so long ago, "the big one" looms as a present danger, so geologists want to shake people up to the dangers.

If you don't like the new moon because you think it's not romantic, just think of it as going through a phase.

When you do computations using the binary number system, you sometimes feel like you don't know the half of it.

Quiet Zone: Any place where there are no cell towers.

Is "chain"-smoking hazardous to your health?

Einstein's family was concerned when he published his work on relativity because they thought it might be an exposé.

At a mathematical conference when the numbers were asked for comments, the zero had nothing to add.

I'm thinking maybe the number "zero" is the introvert of the bunch, while "one" is the extrovert who always has to be first.

In the binary system, the zero is half the story but doesn't add up to much.

Some say the concept of zero is an elegant entity, yet sophisticated in its simplicity. Personally, I think nothing of it.

With nanotechnology, do you think it is possible to create a cell phone for DNA molecules?

I wonder if the steely-eyed civil engineer ever loses his temper.

The meteorologist was so good, his reign on network television lasted thirty years.

When the radiologist went through the x-ray machines at the airport, he got a dose of his own medicine.

When the radiologist went through the x-ray machine at the airport, he felt so exposed.

The hospital instituted random drug testing of all staff. The urologist was especially pissed when he was asked to pee in a cup.

When starting a fire with a match, remember that you're starting from scratch.

When you consult a dermatologist about a rash, you're usually starting from scratch.

The chicken chose mathematics as a profession because he liked that it was eggsact and precise.

After the chicken astronaut retired, she decided to write a memoir about her flight eggsperiences.

The chicken scientist was admonished for eggsagerating the results of her research.

As a scientist and inventor, Jack Rabbit was quite creative, but some thought he was harebrained.

Strong-willed physicists working on semi-conductors often meet resistance from opposing forces.

When the astronaut heifer was launched into orbit, she was the first of the herd shot around the world.

I gave blood today and I don't think my contribution was in vein.

Are elevators considered binary mechanical devices because they either go up or down?

The radiologist got along with his patients because he always tried to see something good in everyone.

When geologists give their reports, you can generally take it for granite their data is rock solid.

Hospitals have several evacuation plans in place to deal with cases of constipation.

Pharmaceutical companies are just vast drug dealers.

Before the knowledge about atoms and sub-atomic particles, nothing was matter-of-fact.

It seems to nuclear physicists that everything matters.

To nuclear scientists, some things do make a particle of difference.

When a nuclear scientist is onto something, it's always "up and atom."

When an experiment starts to get old, nuclear scientists start to look for neutrons.

Nuclear scientists affectionately called the muon the "cat particle."

Nuclear scientists make great partners because they know how to spot small details and express that you matter.

Nuclear physicists are always looking for a little something in their work.

For a nuclear scientist, nothing is ever just a small matter.

Nuclear scientists work in an area of the infinitesimally small. Sometimes they miss what matters.

The science of plate tectonics is the moving story of the origins of modern day continents.

Werner Heisenberg was uncertain in his absoluteness. He just didn't know.

In Werner Heisenberg's experimental findings, things could go either way.

In exasperation about his uncertainty principle, Werner Heisenberg finally just flipped a damned coin.

Werner Heisenberg was known for his razor-sharp mind, but there were some areas where he just wasn't sure.

Among Werner Heisenberg's supporters and detractors, most had difficulty understanding his theories and were never sure.

Werner Heisenberg's Zodiac sign was a question mark.

Even after Werner Heisenberg put forth his theory, he still wasn't absolutely sure.

The scientific community was stunned when Werner Eisenberg published his theory. No one could make heads or tails out of it.

Whether the Large Hadron Collider elicits positive or negative test results really does matter.

The Large Hadron Collider is a 17-mile circular "gun range" shooting two high-energy particles in opposite directions till they collide. What comes out of it matters.

For nuclear scientists working at the Large Hadron Collider, their results are often hit-and-miss.

In the Higgs Boson, nuclear scientists found the "God Particle." Now they need to find her publicist.

When the seismograph was invented, it caused quite a shake-up in the scientific sector.

Geologists like to refer to earthquakes as earth's tribute to rock and roll.

A branch of nuclear science is concerned with understanding the very origin of the universe. They are getting close, but so far there's just a lot of background noise.

When geophysicists initially began describing how the continental plates were moving across the face of the earth, some colleagues initially didn't get the drift.

The meteorologist failed to predict fog in his nightly forecast and explained he simply mist it.

Nuclear scientists are usually taciturn, but when the Higgs Boson was discovered, they radiated their enthusiasm.

Nuclear scientists generally aren't known for their radiant personalities.

The judge issued a restraining order to stop the solar eclipse, but it was disregarded. It then became a matter of investigation of a possible cover up.

Mathematicians love to dance to logarithms, too.

To the surprise of many, the renowned mathematician had written several concertos with a logarithmic beat.

Are grandfather clocks considered a binary device because they go, "tick-tock?"

The mathematician set out to graph "infinity" but didn't know where to begin.

The mathematician's colleagues gave up on the effort to graph "infinity" because they didn't see an end to it.

When geographers start a research project, they first map out all the study's parameters.

When the mathematician and his young wife moved out of the inner city, they bought a place in a subdivision.

When mathematicians gather at conferences, the first thing they do is exchange numbers.

It's a little known fact that the person who starts up the Large Hadron Collider in the morning says, "Beam me up, Scotty."

Physicists working at the Large Hadron Collider are a happy bunch; you can tell because they're always beaming.

In the binary numerical system, the zero doesn't put itself out there, while the one seeks the limelight and always has to be first.

In the binary numerical system, both the one and the zero carry equal weight. It's just that not every number can be number one.

In the binary numerical system, the zero and one are equal, but one adds up to nothing.

Aeronautical engineers love their work. Regardless of some difficult problems to overcome, they still get a lift every day.

Aeronautical engineers say their work isn't just rewarding, it's also just plane fun.

Aeronautical engineers won't take shortcuts because there are dangers associated with winging it.

An aeronautical engineer's work will take off as soon as the company lands a lucrative contract.

The seasoned meteorologist retained a top-level team of attorneys in the hopes of weathering the storm of controversy.

Surviving a long-standing controversy, the meteorologist kept her job as weather anchor because of a flood of support from her fans.

When the Zero family had their first child, they wondered if he would grow up to amount to anything.

When the TV station aired a program on climate change, the station's switchboard was flooded with angry callers.

A Japanese-Italian mathematician was given an honorific title of Pi-San.

The newly graduated hydrologist started his own consulting firm and did extremely well for himself.

The brilliant psychiatrist was told he needed more years of training and experience because he was too Jung.

The senior psychiatrist was exposed for padding his professional resume with Freudulent degrees and awards.

In any serious study of the universe, cosmologists like to start at the beginning.

The deaf physicist discovered a new wrinkle to the old sine wave.

Astronauts have elevated the "mile high club" to even greater heights.

The staid conservative meteorologist got stinking drunk one night and threw caution to the winds.

The deaf mathematician wrote his equations using sine language.

The ASL interpreters at math conferences have developed a friendly sine wave.

When Pluto was downgraded from the category of planet to dwarf planet, it retained celebrity status because it still traveled in the same circles.

You must read all geological research summaries with some skepticism because they almost always are based on faulty data.

When there are problems with the results of a geological study, there is always an effort to determine where the fault lies.

Geologists on the cutting edge of their fields have to be willing to rock the boat.

During the tumultuous 1970s, it was easy for a geologist to get stoned out of his gourd.

Once he started with drugs, the senior geologist slid down the slippery slope until he hit rock bottom.

You wouldn't think a geologist's marriage would be any rockier than anyone else's, but it is said they often quake in their boots.

A geologist's child's worst nightmare is to receive a chunk of coal in his Christmas stocking.

When geologists get older, their bodies go from rock solid to sedimentary.

When the geologist's obsession with the formation of the earth's mantle interfered with his state of mind, his wife wished he could have the plate removed from his head.

Geologists rock!

A group of geologists got together and formed a rock band taking the name "Tectonic Plates." Their musical specialty was the oldies.

On long research digs, geologists pass the time playing the child's game, "rock, paper, scissors."

When geologists find seashells and fossils of ancient sea creatures on mountaintops, they know the area was once ocean front property.

Astronomers as a profession are generally a positive group. They're always looking up.

The meteorologist called in sick because he was feeling a little under the weather.

I hear physicians don't make good patients because they can't take their own medicine.

The invention of the seismograph did shake up the world for geologists. You could say it rocked their world.

The impact of the seismograph affected the work of geologists on a grand scale.

Continental drift was first discussed as early as 1912, but it took a concerted effort to eventually float the idea with scientific bodies.

Climate deniers living in Florida are hedging their bets by investing in boats and flotation devices.

Climate deniers moving to Florida are building their homes on stilts.

Realtors in Florida are anticipating sales to climate deniers by advertising beachfront property 40 miles inland.

In 2006, after careful study, astronomers downgraded Pluto to a dwarf planet. But in some academic orbits, Pluto is still a planet.

Chemists do it because of the chemistry between them.

Physicists do it because of the attraction.

Q: In the classic physics thought experiment, is Schrodinger's cat alive or dead?

A: Yes.

Q: In the classic physics thought experiment, is Schrodinger's cat alive or dead?

A: No.

Schrodinger's cat had another problem. He couldn't make up his mind whether he wanted inside the house or out.

When the operator of the atomic clock was asked if he was ready to start it up he said, "Just a nanosecond."

When the operator of the hourglass was asked if he was prepared to start, he said, "Just a minute."

Astronauts do it in orbit and it's called docking.

Conservationists frequently do it after forest fires and it's called reseeding.

Computer programmers do it and think of it as coding.

Chemists are always experimenting with doing it because they like getting the reactions.

Physicists like to experiment with doing it because they get a charge out of probing the nucleus.

Some in the public believe the banjo is somehow related to string theory.

CHAPTER ELEVEN

EVERYDAY LIFE

When the husband was working on some roof repairs, his wife got upset because she said his mind was in the gutter.

Car crash dummies are indispensable when it comes to crash courses in auto safety.

It should be no surprise that Count Dracula's long distance travels are limited to fly-by-night carriers.

The president of the neighborhood association was mean-spirited and didn't treat people very well, so everyone took to referring to him as the blockhead.

When a lone gunman entered a furniture store and killed a number of people, he was later apprehended and charged with mattresside.

While irritating, it should never come as a surprise when your doctor is late in seeing you; after all, you were asked to sit in the waiting room.

A bank robber's main problem is that he's making unauthorized withdrawals that are frowned upon by the police.

I've been wondering, are prisoners in jails allowed to have cell phones?

Saturday and Sunday are thought of as "rest days." When one retires, what about the rest of the days of the week?

Can a person who's 6'10" be short with you? And don't say "not atall."

Since St. Peter mans the Pearly Gates, does that mean Heaven is a gated community?

The master candle maker created a special line of old scented candles for those who want to wax nostalgically.

If you are an introvert commuter and you take an express train, are you expected to talk with people?

Checkmate: A computer app to help newlyweds balance their finances.

Toupee: Something used to disguise one's hairitage.

Death throes: Your reaction to information you found on the internet about symptoms you have you didn't want to bother your primary care doctor with, and which he said not to look up online.

The inexperienced demonstrator brought a picket fence to the demonstration.

Is it a bad thing to want to prune one's family tree?

When the senior relented and bought himself a smart phone, he was righteously indignant, complaining, "if it's so smart why do I have to do everything to make it work?"

Does chain smoking have a link to lung cancer?

Can a paraplegic be a standup kind of guy?

With the demise of the old dial telephone, why do they still call it a dial tone?

Some airlines have more stringent rules regarding buzzards bringing carrion on longer flights.

The stonemason's daughter rocks!

Arachnophobia is enough to make your skin crawl.

When the millionaire gave his girlfriend a large diamond pin, she cried and said, "You rock!"

The crown chicken decided the smaller yacht was a less eggstravagant show of wealth, even if she'd feel cooped up.

The chicken was an eggspatriot living abroad, until she got homesick and scrambled to come home.

The task was going to be as hard as eggstracting hen's teeth.

The chicken beauty queen discovered that her eggsfoliating cream didn't work; it just ruffled her feathers.

The man asked for a refund on his red-eye flight, saying it was a fly-by-night cheap arrangement.

You'd think people who live in glass houses were all for transparency.

People who live in glass houses should never get stoned.

People who live in glass houses can say curtains to a life of privacy.

If people who live in glass houses weren't known before, their exposure will change all that.

Living in a glass house can be difficult and involve a whole lot of pane.

When you live in a glass house, the matter of privacy can be a pane in the glass.

The mastery and technology that went into the very first Samurai swords was cutting edge.

Whatever you do, don't ever make the mistake of pissing off a urologist.

New parents appreciate their obstetricians because of the responsibilities they've born.

After an argument with his wife, Sam always sits in front of a mirror in order to reflect on his fate.

When Slinky was arrested for going down the stairs under the influence of an intoxicant he knew his family would spring to his defense.

The wrench said to the pliers, "Pinch me, I don't believe it!"

The pliers said to the wrench, "Get a grip. You're losing it!"

The pliers said to the wrench, "Let's grab lunch sometime."

The wrench said to the pliers, "Hold on tight! I'm about to make a sharp turn."

When Sally Tall married Alan Shorter she became Sally Shorter. For Alan he always was Shorter.

When Sally Tall married Alan Shorter she became Shorter. Alan had always been Shorter but Sally newly became Shorter.

When Alan Shorter and Sally Tall Shorter had a baby he was a little Shorter.

If Sally Tall Shorter and Alan Shorter were to have their marriage annulled Alan would still be Shorter but Sally would be Tall again.

Grandma Barbara took a ballpoint pen and snuck up behind grandson, Xander, grabbed him and started writing on her grandson's arm. "Grandma, what are you doing?" "I'm texting you!"

What does it tell us about the intelligence of people who use smart phones while driving?

The "generation gap" shows up in one modern-day statistic: the number of young people who text while driving increases the number of those who won't make it to retirement.

The label "smart phone" is a misnomer: It doesn't turn itself on, does not recognize me, relies on my memory for the password, asks me to give it directions to operate all functions, and badgers me with error messages. And I'm the dumb one?

I'm wondering if "smart phone" refers to how bad it smarts when you have to figure out how the hell it works?

I think it's plain mean to call them "smart phones." It makes me feel so dumb having to figure everything out about it.

Calling it a "smart phone" is a promotional ploy of young developmental engineers who are too smart for their own good.

Some of us remember the saying, "a penny for your thoughts?" In today's economy, that no longer makes cents.

The innovative sleep company specialized in mattresses for the lay public.

Cross-dressing gives some people a sense of identity, whereas for others it can be a drag.

When a mean-spirited bigot comes through checkout and is abusive to the clerk, it is clearly an example of counter terrorism.

Local communities have found that funding the 4th of July fireworks has been difficult because of skyrocketing costs.

Jack-in-the-Box went to see his primary care physician because he'd been feeling jumpy lately.

Jack-in-the-Box was getting so old he lost that spring in his step.

After 10,000 pops, Jack-in-the-Box had to have his spring lubricated.

Jack-in-the-Box's life is never dull. Every time the "weasel goes pop," it's a surprise to him.

The Slinky manufacturer came out with a new line for its spring collection.

A certain segment of today's adults grew up on Sesame Street, just around the corner from Mr. Roger's Neighborhood.

There was a time when all elevators had operators who had learned all the ups and downs of its operation.

The opening session of the OCD conference was delayed because of a typo in the program.

Planning for the OCD conference got bogged down when the rules committee couldn't agree on several compelling issues.

If an extraterrestrial were to visit earth, a hostile reception most likely would make them feel alienated.

The taxi driver left work early because he felt his customers were driving him to distraction.

As far as the IRS is concerned, your finances will never put you at the point of no return.

Once you reach the point of no return, you have no fallback position.

You have a 50% chance of reaching the point of no return.

Once you reach the point of no return, you might as well go ahead with things.

To reach the point of no return, you just need to go halfway. Anything less just won't cut it.

You can still reach the point of no return by a half-hearted attempt.

The Sandman is someone with true grit.

When two egocentric lovers started dating, people said they were an I-tem.

In order to be able to sit for hours in the lotus position, the Buddha had to have a leg up in his physical conditioning.

The long-time TV meteorologist was let go under a cloud of suspicion.

The young couple invested their entire savings in a cattle ranch and steaked their future in its success.

It's always a ticklish situation when the Grammar Police are called in to arrest someone for an indecent preposition.

Should the Grammar Police be called if someone is the object of unwanted prepositioning?

The Grammar Police were alerted to his presence because he was a noun criminal.

Proper nouns expect special treatment by the Grammar Police because of their prominent and lofty station in life.

There is a level of resentment among Grammar Police when dealing with proper nouns because they show such a sense of entitlement.

Grammar Police consider pronouns helpful in identifying nouns. "It" is a big help.

Proper nouns help Grammar Police put a name to a suspect.

Have you noticed that Grammar Police can be short with you, especially if you use a lot of abbreviations?

Period is strong-willed and decisive, whereas his friend, Comma, is more hesitant and pauses when he changes his mind.

Period is headstrong, obstinate even, and goal-driven. Comma is easy-going and casual and pauses to smell the roses.

Companies that produce smart phones have whole departments to promote their sales. Maybe they should be called "sell phones."

How does one open a Surelock Home? The answer, my dear, is simply elementary.

The logical successor to the TV series *The X-Files* is *The Y-Files*. Y indeed? You just have to wait and Z.

Broom married his childhood sweetheart after sweeping her off her feet. They named their firstborn son Whisk.

In the daily status report, the Fashion Police found that suspenders were holding things up.

The crotchety old couple have been married for 40 years in what they describe as a binary relationship: it's off-again, on-again.

The scarecrow spent his days in mindless daydreaming.

The OCD shopper had forgotten what she had written down she needed, so at the grocery store it was difficult because she felt so listless.

The Snow Princess was sick of dating, so she kept giving suitors the cold shoulder.

How does the Snow Princess know when she gets a cold? Does she get a reverse fever?

Psychics, like ordinary people, are notoriously forgetful of their computer passwords. They, however, have access to a psychic hotline where operators are ready to remind callers of their forgotten passwords.

When car manufacturers added automatic transmissions to their cars, they caused many drivers to become shiftless.

Vanity plays a role in people's decision to consult a plastic surgeon because they don't accept their own face value.

When you use your smart phone to call your lover, is it considered a close call?

When the real estate agent concludes a sale on his smart phone, is it considered a close call?

Frosty the Snowman won a vacation trip all expenses paid to Miami, but declined because he didn't want to lose sight of himself.

The Sandman got a little carried away in writing his memoirs and had to admit there was nary a grain of truth to any of it.

Everyone wants to be seen in the best light when they prepare their resume. Sometimes the exaggerations make it hard to see what really lies beneath.

While Casper wasn't an accomplished writer, he decided against going with a ghostwriter for his memoir.

On laundry day, Casper is pretty much homebound because he doesn't have a thing to wear.

If you ask a psychotherapist what kind of music they like, they'll likely tell you they prefer the blues.

Surveys consistently find that the Easter Bunny likes hip-hop music.

The king gave his daughter a girl puppet for her birthday because he wanted to give the little princess a handmaiden.

If you ask what kind of music a true patriot loves, the answer is country.

If you've ever wondered what kind of music weasels like, they prefer pop.

Genealogists are music lovers, too, and their preference is folk.

When traveling in vampire country, always be prepared to stake your life on safety measures.

When confronted with a trick question, a vampire will always bite.

Q: How does a vampire eat after sundown?

A: He takes little bites.

A computer vampire virus wreaks its havoc by messing with little bytes at a time.

When vampires try speed dating, a question that invariably comes up is "What's your type?"

The Hatfield Vampires and the McCoy Vampires had a long-standing blood feud.

The entrepreneur vampire decided to open a blood bank. His business hours were from one hour after sundown to one hour before sunrise.

When the vampire had to have dentures, he also had to switch to eating with an IV.

Vampires aren't hematologists, and when classifying blood types, they often make typeOs.

When it comes to working, vampires prefer the graveyard shift.

Words a vampire doesn't want to hear: "Rise and shine...!"

When vampires travel by air, they usually take the red-eye flight.

Vampires become expert in people-watching in order to take the pulse of potential subjects.

The vampire was a little embarrassed when he was told he was overdrawn at the local blood bank.

There is something very sensual in a vampire nuzzling a woman's neck. For him, it's a move not in vain.

If you're ever in an argument with a vampire, never say in anger, "Bite me...!"

Getting into an argument with a vampire isn't a good thing. You may end up donating blood.

It isn't with a community spirit, but some vampires do have a kind of monthly blood drive.

Q: Why do vampires love family reunions?

A: Because blood is thicker than wine.

Q: What happens when a vampire marries a vampire?

A: They become a blood family.

When it comes to style of music, nuclear physicists tend to like fusion.

Vampires typically aren't gullible. They don't just bite on anything.

Do teenage vampires ever have to wear retainers for an overbite?

Professional repairmen have a curious preference in music. They seem to like Baroque.

When vampires are fatigued, they can get quite snippy and make biting remarks.

Vampires live extremely long lives because it's in their bloodlines.

It's illegal and wrong for cousins to do it, but on some level, it's just a relative matter.

Necking has a very different meaning among vampires.

Vampires join college fraternities because they consider themselves blood brothers.

When on a date with a vampire, be wary if he suggests getting a bite before returning home.

Do retainers work to straighten a vampire's crooked fangs?

Do vampires have to have a degree in hematology because they draw blood?

In your grandfather's day, it didn't take much to switch bad behavior.

When Alice reported what she experienced when she tripped down the rabbit hole, it caused people all over the land to wonder.

The importers of illegal makeup were charged with an attempted cover-up.

When consumers complained about the poor construction quality of the new line of lingerie, the owner offered a flimsy excuse.

Critics of skimpy lingerie often contend that they objectify women, but supporters feel there's nothing to it.

With careful design certain brassieres allow for a plunging neckline, which results in men dropping their eyes.

The maximum amount of cleavage in a brassiere design leaves more than meets the eye.

Contemporary lingerie design often approaches the level of the Emperor's new clothes.

Q: As one ages, bladder problems occasionally become an issue. Is there a satisfactory solution to this problem?

A: Depends.

Q: Do divorce attorneys handle civil cases?

A: The jury is still out on that.

When the hand-held stopwatch was gauged against other timing devices, it was second to none.

When the father of the Light family began studying his family tree, he learned there were a number of dim bulbs on a couple of branches.

The father of the Light family thought of himself as quite a clever fellow, but when it came to telling puns, his family thought he was a dim wit.

Due to privacy and confidentiality matters, when the famous actor underwent orthopedic surgery, the surgical team was kept to a skeleton crew.

In the olden days when you wore holes in your socks, it just meant one more darn task to take care of.

The master clock maker looked forward to retirement because he would have time on his hands.

☺ ☺ ☺

With a watch with a sweep second hand, where's the first?

☺ ☺ ☺

If you base all your news coverage on materials you receive on your fax machine, you're in serious trouble as a news network.

ABOUT THE AUTHOR

© Diana Nagai

Gordon Hideaki Nagai is the author of *The Ultimate Book of Dad Jokes* (Ulysses Press), *The World's 101 Worst Puns* (Nisei Press), and *The World's 101 Next Worst Puns* (Nisei Press). A father and grandfather, he loves creating and sharing jokes with his four grandchildren, Casey, Venice, Xander, and Teiya.

Born in 1938, Gordon is a Nisei, a second generation Japanese-American, whose family owned a farm outside of Atwater, California. His world was abruptly changed on December 7, 1941, when Japan attacked Pearl Harbor. Thus began a chain of events that resulted in his family's forced evacuation and internment in an internment camp in Colorado during the war.

After the war, Gordon spent his teenage years in school and working on the family farm. He graduated from UC Berkeley in 1960 and earned a masters in social welfare in 1963. He worked in a variety of social service settings, the last as a case manager for developmentally challenged clients in San Mateo, San Francisco, and Marin Counties.

When his wife retired, they moved to Eugene, Oregon, following their children and grandchildren.